KT-169-514

Introduction
By Professor Robert Winston

Imagine if the hugs, lullabies and smiles you give to your baby could inoculate him against the first heartbreaks, 'tricky-teenager' tendencies and even help with exams decades later. Evidence from a new branch of science is showing that this might even be possible after all.

The human brain is made up of over 100 billion neurons or brain cells, each of which connect to more than 2,000 other neurons. Every one of us has connections that are more complex than the London, New York and Tokyo telephone exchanges put together. And this mass of tissue is where we think, see, move, enjoy, get angry, feel sadness, remember and love. Our brains are the most intricate objects in the known universe.

Your baby's brain is both complicated and vulnerable, and the experiences your baby has during this period create millions of new connections. Babies who experience insufficient love, laughter and stimulation will stunt the potential development of their brains.

Human babies are born more immature than other mammals – calves can stand on four legs less than an hour after birth. Our babies take around a year to learn to stand and walk and even then need so much protection for years ahead. Parenting is more important than we could ever have imagined. Although I have published over 300 research papers in scientific journals, I have no doubt my most important achievement is my own three children. And all of us in different ways are capable of contributing to that next generation.

As parents we can worry so much about things that just aren't as important to our children, such as giving them their own room, buying them toys and taking them on holidays. Actually, the most valuable gift you can give to your child is free: it's simply your love, time and support.

This is no empty sentiment – scientific research is now demonstrating why a baby's brain needs love more than anything else. The science of epigenetics (the study of chemical reactions and the factors that influence them) is discovering how our genes are affected by our environment and thus how our brain is affected by the lives we lead. For example, studies show that young mice with loving mothers, who are attentive and lick them caringly, grow up to be better mothers themselves when they have pups, and these children are more intelligent and more sociable. This effect is so strong that it can stretch over two generations – and possibly more. Young mice may become better mothers and be able to cope with stress better too, all because their grandmother took good care of their mother. These long-lasting benefits of good parenting are dependent on chemical alterations in the DNA. These same staggering changes in the brains of mice and other animals have also now been confirmed in humans.

I have worked for decades on early development and this science is demonstrating what so many of us have always felt: that depriving children of a loving family environment causes lasting damage to their emotional well-being, their intelligence and their capacity to develop fully. It is for this reason that I have become involved in this guide. We hope this book (www.essentialparent.com) will help answer all your questions and help you feel more confident as a parent.

Chapter 1: Breastfeeding

The evidence of the benefits of breastfeeding to both mother and baby, and the risks of not breastfeeding, are well-established. Breastfeeding has a positive impact on mother-baby relationships, and this strong early relationship and a stable and loving environment are known to help a baby's early health and emotional, social and physical development in later life.

Breastfeeding is a skill that every new mum can learn but it takes practice. There are basic techniques and feeding positions to master. Ask your midwife or health visitor or talk to a breastfeeding consultant.

Understanding the importance of skin-to-skin contact, your baby's tummy size and the types of milk your breasts produce are all good to know. There's a lot to learn!

What are the benefits of breastfeeding?

Breastfeeding has some of the most wide-reaching and long-lasting effects on a baby's health and development. Healthcare professionals around the world and the UK Department of Health agree that it's best to breastfeed your baby exclusively for the first six months, if you can. Breastmilk not only meets all of your baby nutritional needs, but there are a lot of benefits for you as well.

Benefits to your baby
- It is perfectly formulated for your baby's needs and changes as she develops.
- The antibodies in your breastmilk will protect your baby from infection in the early days. She will be less likely to develop childhood illnesses such as asthma and eczema.

- Breastmilk contains the hormone melatonin and an amino acid called tryptophan, both essential for sleep.
- Your baby is less likely to suffer from gastric infections (gastroenteritis or rotorvirus), respiratory infections, allergies (asthma or lactose intolerance) or long-term diseases such as diabetes or obesity.
- It is available whenever and wherever your baby needs to be fed and delivered at the perfect temperature.
- It is easy to digest, so babies are less likely to spit up, suffer wind or become constipated.
- It improves strength of premature babies.
- Skin-to-skin contact during feeding helps regulate your baby's temperature and heartbeat.
- It makes for an easier transition to solid foods as the flavour of your breastmilk changes according to the foods that you eat.

Benefits to you

- It helps with bonding – the hormones, including oxytocin, that you produce when you are breastfeeding help bonding.
- It's free – all you need are a couple of nursing bras, some nursing pads and possibly a feeding pillow.
- There is no feeding equipment to carry when you are out and about.
- Night-time feeds are much easier and far less disruptive to your sleep and your baby's – no fumbling in the dark to make up a bottle.
- Oxytocin encourages your uterus to contract back to its pre-pregnancy size; it triggered uterine contractions during the birth and continues to do so while feeding. Oxytocin also promotes sleep.
- It helps you to lose your pregnancy weight – breastfeeding and milk production burn 500 calories each day.
- It reduces your risk of breast and ovarian cancers.

What is breast milk and is it always the same?

Breastmilk is the perfect food for your baby. It not only changes during a single feed, but it also alters to meet your baby's needs as he grows. It's vital to understand your milk and the way your baby feeds, for your baby's health and to keep your milk supply going.

What is colostrum?

For the first few days after the birth, your breasts produce a special yellow-coloured, highly concentrated fluid called colostrum; midwives often call it 'liquid gold'. It contains everything a newborn baby needs for nutrition and it's packed with your antibodies to protect the baby from infection. It can really help your baby's immature tummy and protect it from serious diseases.

When will mature milk begin?

Your breasts start producing mature milk about three days after the birth of your baby – it is thinner than colostrum and produced in much greater quantities. The more often you try to feed in the first days, the more signals you will give to your body to start making it. Around day three your breasts will start to feel heavier and fuller, and they'll look much bigger too; mature breastmilk production has begun. It may take a little bit longer if your baby was early, or if you had a Caesarean. Talk to your midwife or health visitor if you're concerned. The key to getting milk production going is to keep trying.

Breastmilk changes during a feed. To begin with you produce foremilk, a thinner liquid that quenches your baby's thirst. As the feed goes on, your baby will eventually reach the hindmilk; midwives call this the 'pudding' because it's thick and rich. Hindmilk is more concentrated and high in fat, essential for your baby's nutrition and development, and will also keep your baby fuller for longer.

So don't switch breasts halfway through a feed, or your baby will just have two lots of foremilk. This might lead him to have diarrhoea, or explosive green poos (see page 87) – but more importantly he may still be hungry. Let your baby feed as long as he wants on one breast so he gets enough of the filling hindmilk. Top up from the other breast at the end of the feed if necessary.

How do I know if my baby is getting what he needs?

The rhythm of a baby's sucking changes slightly throughout a feed. To begin with, while your baby is drinking the foremilk, the sucks are usually quite long and slow. Your baby may take little breaks, but then will go back to the long, slow rhythm.

Once he starts feeding on the thicker hindmilk, he will start tiny little sucks that are quite fluttery. Some mums will misinterpret this and think their baby is finished and simply playing, but those little fluttery sucks are very efficient at getting the nutritious "pudding". So let your baby keep going until he really shows you he's finished.

How does breastfeeding work?

Newborn babies are ready to feed pretty much right after birth. Skin-to-skin contact will encourage your baby to search for your breast and have her first feed. When your baby lies on your chest she can smell your skin, which encourages her natural instinct to suckle. At this first feed your baby will be getting the very rich first 'milk' called colostrum.

After two or three days your 'mature milk' will begin to come in (see page 8). However, it takes a few weeks for breastfeeding to become established, so you will need to feed your baby fairly frequently, including throughout the night, during these first weeks. If you don't do this, your breasts won't get the signal to make enough milk.

Breastfeeding is all about supply and demand. If your baby feeds a lot, your breasts will make more milk. If your baby isn't feeding much, your supply will start to reduce pretty quickly. To begin with, even if you feel like your baby isn't getting much milk, let her feed as much she wants, so your breasts will get the signals they need to produce the right amount of milk for your baby's needs.

How do I latch my baby on to breastfeed?

Pregnant mums often think breastfeeding will be really simple. And for some of them (the lucky ones) it is. For most new mums, there's quite a lot of learning and practising involved. Like any new skill, it takes time and there can be some bumps in the road, but the health benefits of breastfeeding for you and your baby make it worth a very good try.

Talking to your midwife or health visitor, watching an experienced mum, watching our online courses and/or having a lesson with a breastfeeding consultant will make it even easier.

What's the right position for the baby's mouth?

If you feel the roof of your mouth with your tongue you should find a soft, squishy bit at the back. This is where the nipple should be in your baby's mouth. If your nipple ends up on the baby's hard palate it can get sore for you.

How should I hold my baby?

The most important thing is to support your baby's neck and shoulders (not the head), so that he is free to throw his head back and come in towards the breast chin first. Try to get your baby in really close and in a nice straight line, facing the breast and free to tilt his head back.

How do I know he's latched on?

You will need to learn to just wait until your baby's mouth is really wide open and at that point you have to be quite quick and bring him close to your nipple. If he opens his mouth wide and throws his head back, he will come into the breast chin first. The baby will be able to scoop up a really big mouthful of breast and your nipple will end up on that soft cushion at the back of the his mouth.

If your baby is properly attached at the breast you shouldn't feel any pain. It may feel odd when he first latches on, but after ten seconds or so it won't hurt if your nipple has been drawn into the soft cushion area at the back of your baby's mouth. Your baby will look like he has big cheeks because his mouth is full of your breast. There should be a steady sucking rhythm. You could be able to hear your baby swallowing milk. If it is uncomfortable, he may not be latched on properly. Gently pop your little finger into the side of his mouth to break the latch and start again.

Can my baby breathe when he's feeding?

Lots of mothers worry that their baby will find it difficult to breathe if his nose is pressed against a full breast. But if your baby is free to throw back his head every so often then he will simply just pull himself off you if he can't breathe. That's one of the main reasons for you not to hold your baby too tightly. Let him have some freedom of movement.

BREASTFEEDING TIPS

Make yourself comfortable as you are likely to be sitting in the same place for a while and ensure that you have everything to hand.

- Hold your baby close, supporting her neck but allowing her head to move.
- Position your baby so that her nose is opposite your nipple and her head is free to tilt back.
- Bring her towards the breast with her chin in first.
- Wait for your baby to open her mouth really wide.
- Let your baby take a big mouthful of breast so that your nipple just slips under her upper lip; don't push your breast into her mouth. She should start to feed.
- If your baby isn't attached properly, insert your little finger gently into the side of her mouth to break the latch, then start again.

What are the most popular positions for breastfeeding?

You can feed your baby in any position that you find comfortable and each baby and mum will work out what is best for them. When you start, it's a good idea to experiment with different positions, and sometimes you might need to change to help overcome a problem like mastitis (see page 19). It's a good idea to alternate feeding positions sometimes to help prevent blocked ducts. Whichever position you use, try to be relaxed and don't lift and push your breast into your baby's mouth. It's important that you are comfortable when you feed too. You may want to have a pillow under your baby to lift her nearer the breast, especially in the early days when she is very small.

Cradle hold

This is the traditional hold that you see most mums using. The baby's body is across the front of yours – her tummy against your tummy – facing the breast. Cradle the baby close to your body with your arm.

Make sure that your baby's head is free to tilt back. The cradle hold is quite a nice position as you've got quite a lot of control over what the baby's doing. You need to wait until your baby opens her mouth really, really wide then bring in towards you to latch on to the breast.

Underarm or rugby hold

With this position support your baby's body and shoulders along the arm of the side you are feeding on so her head is at the breast. It can help to have a pillow under your arm to support your baby's weight. Your baby needs to start off with her nose near your nipple so her mouth can take a big mouthful of breast and nipple when she latches on.

The rugby hold is a good position if you are tandem-feeding twins because you can have one baby under each arm. It is also useful if you have had a Caesarean (it keeps the weight off your wound), if you have very big breasts, or you have a toddler and want a free hand to play with her while you are feeding. Try this position if you have a blocked duct on one side of your breast as your baby will massage it as she feeds as well as draining the breast, which can help clear the blockage.

Biological nurturing position or laid-back position

The biological nurturing position is one where you lie back with your baby on your chest and let her help herself. This position relies on your baby's instinct to do the right thing, which is really strong. This position can be really lovely after the birth when you are both in skin-to-skin contact and your baby has a strong rooting instinct and tries to almost crawl to the breast. It's only really a good one for at home on the sofa or in bed.

When you lie down gravity helps the baby to latch on properly. The aim is to have no gaps between your bodies. For this breastfeeding position ideally you need head support: for example, reclined on your sofa. Your baby needs complete body contact from her chest to her feet as this triggers her natural feeding instincts.

Lying on your side
Lying down is a good breastfeeding position for evening and night feeds. Start on your side with your baby facing you, tummy to tummy, so that her nose is level with your nipple. In this position a baby should take a lot of breast tissue from underneath your nipple into her mouth. This position is also good if you think you have a blocked duct in lobes at the bottom of your breast. It is also a great feeding position if you've had a Caesarean, because your baby's weight is not on your wound.

Can every woman breastfeed?

Most mums can breastfeed, but it's a learned skill and some need more help to get going. If you're ever struggling, watch our online course, talk to your midwife, health visitor, or other mums. Find out where your local breastfeeding group or breastfeeding counsellor service is based.

Will I have enough milk?
The body adjusts its milk supply to a baby's needs each day. Very few mums can't produce the right amount, but it is important to understand that it may take a few days to build it up. The trick to getting it going quickly is to feed your baby little and often through the day and night. This will stimulate the milk supply.

Correct attachment will stimulate your breasts to make enough milk for your baby. If you are concerned your baby isn't latched on properly, ask your midwife, health visitor or local breastfeeding support group to check. They know what to look for and can teach you too.

Will I be able to breastfeed with small breasts?
Yes. Both large-breasted and small-breasted women will notice that their breasts get bigger and heavier when they begin feeding. This is due to an increase in breast tissue and presence of milk in the breast.

Will I be able to breastfeed with flat nipples?
Nipples come in all shapes, sizes and colours. Your baby is not expecting a certain kind of nipple; yours are the only ones he will know. Whatever shape nipple you have, it should be possible to breastfeed provided your baby is properly latched on (see page 9).

Can I breastfeed if I'm taking drugs or medication?

A small number of mums, although they would like to breastfeed, cannot do so for medical reasons. If you are on medication for a long-term condition, check with your pharmacist and/or talk to your doctor about whether you might be able to change your medication. It's important to consider the risks of not breastfeeding, for the mother, the baby and the family. The Breastfeeding Network provides a list of alternative medications that are safe to use while breastfeeding.

Will I be able to breastfeed if I have had breast surgery?

Breast surgery, breast implants and breast-reduction surgery can all affect the chances of breastfeeding. If you have had surgery and would like to breastfeed, speak to your surgeon to find out more about the procedure you had and its effects on breastfeeding.

If one breast has had surgery or been removed, it is possible to breastfeed a baby on just one side and your breast will be able to build an adequate milk supply for your baby. The same applies if you have had a nipple removed from one breast.

Is bonding possible if I can't breastfeed?

Don't worry; you can still bond with your baby if you are bottle-feeding her. You can still have skin-to-skin contact by taking off your shirt when you're feeding at home and you will get to know your baby's feeding cues. Try to replicate the feeling of breastfeeding as much as you can, and the bond won't be affected.

How do I know when my baby is hungry?

New mums often worry that they are feeding their babies either too often or not enough. Babies give lots of signals to let you know they're hungry and it can be really helpful to learn to spot your baby's feeding cues. You will begin to recognise these cues and distinguish hunger from other signals. Signs that a baby is hungry include:

- urgent sucking on a blanket, his fist, your finger or even your face;
- licking his lips;

- opening his mouth a little bit;
- searching and 'rooting' for your breast when you hold him.

Does it help to have a feeding routine?

UNICEF UK Baby Friendly breastfeeding experts don't recommend enforcing a routine. They suggest it's better to follow your baby's lead – known as feeding on demand. All babies are different. Some want quite frequent feeds – every two to three hours – for several weeks; others start to space out their feeds after a couple of weeks.

As your milk supply becomes established and your baby becomes more settled you'll gradually notice that she develops her own feeding pattern. Feeds may become shorter and easier as you both become more efficient. Your baby might feed very quickly and request a feed every four hours on the dot or she may always cluster-feed in the evening and then do a big long stretch of sleep at night. Then just when you think you have a pattern you will have a few days when she's back to feeding all day. As your baby grows, you will learn to follow her feeding cues. Your baby will tell you when she's hungry and also when she's had enough. If you're well attuned to these cues, and your baby is well latched on to feed, you can time the feeds around them.

How do I know my baby is getting enough milk?

Most mums worry whether their baby is getting enough milk. The easiest ways to tell are these simple guidelines:

- In the first 48 hours there should be two to three wet nappies;
- After three to four days your baby should have about six wet nappies a day;
- By day four to five your baby should be starting to produce yellow poo (see pages 87-88) at least two per day;
- Your baby is gaining weight;
- Your baby looks healthy and alert.

If you are concerned, take your baby to be weighed regularly. The health visitor will plot the weight on a graph in the red book. If his weight gain is steady, he is getting enough milk. If your baby does not have enough wet nappies contact your GP immediately, as it's potentially dangerous for a baby to become dehydrated.

How much breastmilk does a baby drink?
Your baby will drink enough to fill his stomach. It's difficult to give a precise amount as it can't be measured, but it will probably be a lot less than you think as a baby's stomach is very small. A newborn's stomach is about the size of a small marble; by the time he's a month old it's about the size of a ping-pong ball. You will know when your baby has had enough as he will usually spit out the nipple, he may look sleepy or even drunk or may be calm and look around. If he is still awake offer him the other breast. He may want some of it or none of it.

How long does a normal feed last?

In the very early days your baby will want to have a lot of feeds; some longer, some shorter. A feed may be only a few minutes or up to an hour. The frequent feeds are really important because they give your body messages to make milk. A baby who is feeding efficiently will get all the milk she needs much more quickly than one who isn't attached properly. So if your baby is taking a long time to feed and doesn't seem to be satisfied for at least couple of hours after that feed, check that she is latching on properly (see pages 9-10).

Do I need to wind my baby after a feed?

Some babies need winding; others don't. You will learn what your baby needs very quickly. Start by winding your baby part-way through a feed; sit him up or hold him against your shoulder and rub his back gently. He may bring up wind, or he may want to continue feeding. Put a muslin against your shoulder just in case some milk comes up with the wind.

Do I need to offer my baby water?

No, you don't, as long as you let your baby breastfeed whenever she wants to. Thirst is quenched by foremilk, and your body makes more foremilk when it is hot. This may mean extra feeds in hot weather.

What happens in a growth spurt?

Don't worry if your baby suddenly changes his feeding pattern and wants to be fed more often again. Just like when you were pregnant, he grows in spurts. Often at around six weeks lots of mums think their milk supply has decreased because their babies are feeding every two hours again. Don't worry. When your baby feeds more than usual, he sends a message to your breasts to make more milk. This feeding behaviour during a growth spurt generally lasts for 24 to 48 hours and then everything settles down again.

What are cluster feeds?

This is a term that describes how, at a particular time of day, often in the late afternoon or early evening, babies want lots of feeds close together. The helpful thing about cluster feeding is that your baby may then have a good long sleep when she goes to sleep at bedtime!

Does a breastfed baby need vitamin supplements?

Breastmilk includes all the nutrients a baby needs. However, it is recommended that pregnant and breastfeeding women take a vitamin D supplement to ensure that their baby is born with enough stores to last them until six months of age. If you did not take a supplement during pregnancy and are exclusively breastfeeding, your child may be at risk of vitamin D deficiency and may need a vitamin supplement from the age of one month. Talk to your health visitor or doctor to find out if you, or your baby, are at risk.

How can I make night feeding easier?

Newborn babies have tiny stomachs that are only about the size of a small marble. As a result they need feeding throughout the night. Their tummies fill up fast, but they empty quickly too and a small baby can become dehydrated very easily. To promote your milk supply, you need to feed little and often to keep the feedback loops in your body going.

If you've spent all your adult life with blissful uninterrupted sleep, then having to wake up several times in the night can be really exhausting. The good news is that there are several things you can do to make night feeds less disruptive for everyone.

Sharing a bedroom with your baby

Your baby needs to be in the same room as you for at least the first six months. The Department of Health recommend this as a way to protect your baby from sudden infant death syndrome (SIDS – see page 49). One of the best ways to do this without disrupting your own sleep (or your partner's) too much is to have a cot with a drop-down side, pushed up against the side of your bed. It means that you will be able to reach out and pick your baby up for a feed as soon as she wakes. If she's in another room, she'll have to cry to get your attention.

Can I lie down to feed my baby?

You can feed your baby lying on your side or on your back. Night feeding can be much easier as you can lie down on your bed. If your baby's cot is beside your bed, you can pick her up to feed, then simply slide her back into her cot afterwards and you can go back to sleep.

Are there benefits to breastfeeding at night?

Getting up in the night to breastfeed your baby is tough. All new parents feel tired and sleep deprived, but breastfeeding mums who feed their babies at night enjoy several advantages:

- Breastfeeding mums produce lots of oxytocin during a night feed, which helps them drop off to sleep more quickly afterwards.
- Prolactin (the hormone that instructs the breast to make milk) levels peak in the night so babies get really nourishing feeds.

- Breastmilk contains both melatonin (a hormone) and tryptophan (an amino acid, or protein), which promote sleep in babies.
- Studies have reported that breastfeeding mums get an extra 45 minutes of sleep in the first months compared to mums and dads who are bottle feeding, as they don't have to make up bottles.
- Breastfeeding at night promotes and maintains milk supply, which increases the chances of successful breastfeeding.
- Sharing a room with their parents and rousing for night feeds helps to protect babies from SIDS.

How can I encourage my baby to sleep through the night?

Your main objective is to teach your baby the difference between day and night feeds. Keep everything calm and quiet and chat less in the night feed so he understands that the night feed is just about feeding.

What are the most common breastfeeding problems?

Most of the common breastfeeding problems can be traced back to poor attachment. Once you get that latch right, problems such as mastitis or blocked ducts won't come up. If you experience any of these, try to get some expert help quickly to sort out your latch, so you can avoid it happening again. Also, learn the great skill of hand-expressing, since that will help you out of many tricky situations.

Mastitis

This is an inflammation in your breast tissues. If not treated quickly, an infection can develop. Mastitis can be caused by a build-up of milk in your breast (for example, when milk first comes in or because of poor attachment) or cracked nipples becoming infected.

You might feel an inflamed lump in your breast or areas of your breasts might be red, hot, painful, hard and swollen. You may also experience flu-like symptoms, such as chills, headache, exhaustion and raised temperature.

What to do If you have a fever, an infection may have developed, call your doctor as you will need a course of antibiotics. Feed more frequently than usual so that the milk does not build up. Drink lots of water. Reduce the pain by taking the recommended dose of ibuprofen or paracetamol – it is safe to breastfeed with these. Don't stop feeding – the build-up of milk will make it worse, and feeding from an infected breast won't harm the baby. If the pain is too much, express your milk and feed it to your baby in a bottle. Try feeding with the rugby hold – changing positions can really help. Start a feed from the unaffected breast first. Leave your breast exposed after a feed so that it dries naturally – wash with only water – no soap.

Blocked ducts

If you develop a lump in your breast, with a red, tender patch on the skin, it might be what's called a 'blocked duct', although in fact the duct might not actually be blocked, but the tissue around it has become swollen, which can press on it. True blocked ducts are more rare and tend to occur once you've been breastfeeding for a while; a small white spot at the end of your nipple can be a sign that the duct opening has become blocked by skin cells growing over it.

What to do First try to massage and/or hand express to free the duct. You can also try changing the position your baby feeds with. If neither is helping, talk to your health visitor or doctor, as it's possible there's an infection that needs treatment. The best way to prevent blocked ducts is to make sure that your baby is latched on properly.

Blebs

A bleb is a pressure cyst that occurs when a tiny amount of milk seeps into the nipple tissue at a duct outlet, and it is generally the result of an improper latch. Blebs usually have an irregular shape and stay flat when pressure is applied to the nipple stem. Although blebs are generally painless, some women experience pinpoint pain when they breastfeed.

What to do Apply a warm compress between feeds to soothe any discomfort. Make sure that your baby latches on properly when you are feeding.

Oral thrush

This is a common condition that affects about one in 20 babies. It's most common in babies in the first eight weeks as young babies are still developing their immune systems. Premature babies (born before 37 weeks) are more likely to develop thrush because of their undeveloped immune systems. Sometimes mum has it as well and it can be passed back and forth between mum and baby. Exhausted mums who are breastfeeding can be quite run down and are prone to infection. Also a newborn may have picked up thrush during a normal vaginal delivery.

Signs that your baby might have thrush include: cottage-cheese-like or milky-looking deposits in the baby's mouth that don't come off when you rub them gently; upset or fussy baby feeding; white, shiny saliva; red or spotty face; red, sore bottom, like a nappy rash. If you develop thrush from your baby you may notice sore nipples or an infected area of breast as well; if so, talk to your doctor.

What to do Thrush may go away on its own after a day or two. If it does not talk to your GP, who may give your baby some antifungal cream (for the rash) and/or drops. You will also need to be checked to prevent a cycle of mother-to-baby-and-back infection.

Sore nipples

Sore, cracked or bleeding nipples are usually caused by poor attachment when feeding, thrush (see above), or tongue-tie, below.

What to do If sore nipples have been caused by poor attachment, talk to your midwife or health visitor, or see a breastfeeding counsellor to check that your baby is latching on properly. Breast pads can be useful if you need a little soft padding.

Tongue-tie

Some babies are born with a thread of skin joining the underside of the tongue to the bottom of the mouth. In some cases the tongue may almost fuse to the bottom of the mouth. These babies may not be able to attach properly to the breast.

What to do If your baby has mild tongue-tie, it may not affect her. If severe or it is causing feeding difficulty, the piece of skin can be cut with a simple quick procedure (frenulectomy) under local or general anaesthetic. Your midwife, health visitor or breastfeeding counsellor can advise whether treatment is necessary.

Can I feed with engorged breasts?

If your breasts are very full and hard, your baby may have difficulty latching on, and when he does it can be painful for you at first. The trick here is to express some milk by hand before he starts feeding so your breasts are relaxed again. Pat the breast dry with a muslin after expressing so it's not too slippery for your baby to latch on. Another option is feeding from above. Lay your baby on a flat surface like a mattress, then crouch over him in a comfortable position so your nipple meets your baby's nose. Then the baby can scoop the nipple and lots of breast tissue into his mouth.

How and when do I stop breastfeeding?

When you stop breastfeeding is very much up to you. The UK Department of Health, UNICEF UK Baby Friendly, paediatricians and midwives all agree that exclusive breastfeeding for the first six months is best, if possible. However, you can keep going for longer if you like. In many countries it's not unusual to breastfeed for up to two years or longer. You may want to stop if you are going back to work. However, you can continue breastfeeding when you return to work by providing expressed milk for your baby.

Whatever you decide to do, depending on your baby's age, it's a good idea to make the change gradually. In any case, your baby is unlikely to let you make a quick change since she will be very keen to continue breastfeeding. You also need to let your body respond slowly to the signals that your baby is feeding less often, and your supply can start to reduce. Some breastfed babies don't like a bottle – so make the change with expressed milk first – or try with a soft-spouted beaker – whatever she prefers is fine. Once your baby is used to the bottle or a beaker with expressed milk, then you can gradually switch to water and formula.

Can I mix breastfeeding and formula-feeding?

You might have decided that you will partly breastfeed your baby and partly formula-feed him. In this case, your milk supply will reduce over time. It might not happen quickly since your breasts will initially be expecting your baby to be breastfeeding. So you may need to express milk just to prevent your breasts from becoming hard and engorged – but not too much or it will have the reverse affect.

You might find that you want to introduce just one bottle of formula, but end up increasing the number of bottles each day for several reasons: your milk supply reduces, your baby's hunger and fullness patterns change, or your baby simply refuses breastfeeds (especially if he was having problems breastfeeding) as milk drips more easily into his mouth passively from a bottle – your baby has to work harder for a breastfeed as it uses more muscles.

Are there any risks of giving breast and formula-feeds?

The short answer is yes. Breast milk is the best food for your baby; just having less can affect development. Breastfeeding works on a supply-and-demand system. So if you start swapping breastfeeds for formula feeds, especially in the early weeks after birth, you will reduce your milk supply just as your baby will start to demand more. You're effectively jeopardising your chances of being able to continue to breastfeed.

Does introducing formula milk affect your baby's gut?

Colostrum and mature breastmilk line your baby's gut with a protective layer that promotes the development of gut flora and optimal immune health. Many studies suggest that this has long-term benefits as it can reduce the risk of allergies, eczema and asthma. The more breastmilk your baby has, the greater these benefits. Formula milk does not provide this protection and mixing formula and breastfeeding may interrupt this process.

Will combined feeding or mixed feeding give my baby more milk?

Not necessarily, as your body will produce less. If you are worried about how much milk your baby is getting, it is better for his long-term health to try and build up your milk supply (by feeding little and often) – rather than supplement her breastfeeds with formula milk. If you are concerned about your milk supply or your baby's growth, talk to your health visitor or doctor or go to your breastfeeding drop-in clinic.

Can I switch back to exclusive breastfeeding from mixed feeding?
You might have tried formula-feeding and want to switch back to breastfeeding. This is usually quite difficult, since your body has had signals to stop or reduce milk production, but it is possible. The main thing to remember is that it will take some time and it's worth persevering. Follow all the same guidelines as for early breastfeeding, feeding little and often, and your milk supply should build up again.

Is there any benefit to mixed feeding versus formula feeding?
Your baby will benefit hugely even from a little breastfeeding. If you are going back to work you can offer him a breastfeed before you leave for work and then a feed when you get home, and then – depending on his age and stage – feeding at night will stimulate your supply. His carer can then feed formula during the day; better still, express your milk while you are at work, then no mixed feeding is necessary. The benefits to partial breastfeeding include:

- nutritional benefits;
- disease, allergy-prevention, immunological benefits – the more breastmilk, the greater the benefit, even 50 ml (2 fl oz) of breastmilk per day will help to promote good health;
- bonding and skin-to-skin benefits;
- improved oral development (breastfeeding develops the facial muscles).

What if I'm returning to work and I can't breastfeed my baby as often?

If you're returning to work, switching from breastfeeding to bottle-feeding may be the only option, certainly during the week. However, you can express your milk, so that it can be fed to your baby when you are out. Express some at home and find a private spot at work to express. This will ensure you maintain all the benefits of breastmilk and keep up your supply.

How do I stop breastfeeding when I start weaning my baby?

Try to do this slowly if your baby is reluctant to stop breastfeeding – remember it's a source of great comfort to him, so try not to rush things. There are a few stages to go through, which include:

- Let your baby finish a full breastfeed, then offer him a small amount of food – such as a purée, or something to chew. Your baby will still receive most of his nourishment from breastmilk, but you can both have fun with different tastes and textures.
- Once your baby has started to eat well, you can start to reduce the number of feeds. At some mealtimes, try offering food before you breastfeed.
- The last step is to offer your baby water in a soft-spouted beaker, instead of a breastfeed.

If I switch to formula-feeding, how can I stop my milk production?

Stop gradually so your body will receive the signals to stop producing so much milk. A good idea is to stop one feed at a time as your supply runs down. If your breasts become engorged you need to hand/pump express a little to relieve the pressure. But don't express too much; otherwise your supply will continue to build up.

What are the benefits of expressing milk?

Expressing milk means squeezing milk out of your breast – using either your hand or a manual/electric pump. There are lots of reasons why you might want to do this. Common ones are so that your partner can feed your baby occasionally without having to introduce a bottle of formula, if you go back to work, or you are going to be away from your baby for a while but you want to continue breastfeeding. Expressing serves two purposes. Firstly, it lets you empty your breasts through the day, just as you would if you were feeding your baby, so they don't become engorged. Doing this ensures that your milk supply doesn't decrease. Secondly, it means that your baby can continue to have expressed milk when you are not there.

Expressing breastmilk is also really useful if you have engorged breasts (see page 22) and it hurts when your baby starts to feed. In this case, you can just hand-express a little milk first, so your breast isn't too hard and full. Being able to hand express is also useful if think you are developing mastitis (see page 19). Some gentle hand-expressing will massage the blockage in the duct.

How do I express milk?

Just like breastfeeding, expressing is a skill that takes practice. There are two ways to express breastmilk: hand-expressing or using a pump. When you breastfeed your baby, your baby just being there next to you starts all the right hormones flowing to get the milk to come down. If you're expressing at work when your baby is not with you, those hormones and the milk won't flow. You can 'trick' the hormones by thinking about your baby, imagining her with you, having a picture of your baby near you, and so on. You'll find out what works for you to get your milk flowing.

The first and most vital thing is to start practising well before you need to be doing it for real. It takes a while to get the hang of and you don't want to be worrying about it on your first day back at work!

Hand-expressing

This method is better if you don't need to express a lot of milk, or you are relieving a blocked duct. Some people find it helps to put a warm flannel on the breasts or even lie in a warm bath. To start expressing, put your fingers in a 'C' shape and find the right spot – usually around 2 cm (¾ inch) back from the base of your nipple. When you bring your thumb and your forefinger together with a little squeeze, milk comes out. Eventually you'll get a few drips, your drips will become squirts… and there you go. Make sure you catch the milk in something clean.

Go all the way round your breast, and then onto the other breast; then if you still need a bit more milk, go back to the first side again. Keep doing it until you've got enough.

Using a breast pump

When you need serious quantities of milk to actually feed your baby, then a manual or mechanical pump is much quicker and more effective. There are two main kinds of pump: hand pumps and battery-operated or electric pumps. Try them both out and see which you like best. With an electric breastpump, you put the round plastic shield over your breast, turn the pump on, and it does all the work. It takes around 15 minutes to pump both breasts. Expressing takes longer with a manual pump – around 45 minutes – since you have to pump the milk yourself. Start with the suction on the lowest level and turn it up as you get used to it. As with hand-expressing, it can take some time to learn how to use a pump. Remember to sterilise all the parts after use.

The same ideas for getting the hormones and the milk flowing that we talked about for hand-expressing also work for pump-expressing. So if you haven't got the baby with you, try thinking about her, looking at a baby photo, or massaging your breast with something like a warm flannel first. This will help the hormones to flow, and then just use the pump following the instructions. Practice is the key.

How can I store breastmilk?

You can store your expressed breastmilk at room temperature for up to six hours or in a cool box with ice packs for up to 24 hours. You can keep it in the fridge for up to five days (but don't put it in the door as this is the warmest part of the fridge). Breastmilk can be kept in the fridge's freezer compartment for two weeks or in a freezer for up to six months.

Do I need to sterilise the equipment?

Yes, you need to follow the same routine as for bottle-feeding (see chapter 2, pages 33-34).

How do you switch from breast to bottle?

As with most things to do with babies – it's different for all of them! Some babies seem not to even notice switching over. Others will put up a determined fight. You may need to try different teats, which is really a matter of trial and error. Generally a slow-flow teat is good to start with, since the speed with which milk comes though a fast-flow teats might overwhelm your baby. Remember babies have to suck pretty hard on your breast to get the milk, so they're used to slow flow. Don't be surprised if it takes a long time – babies are programmed to breastfeed and they need to learn new skills to bottle-feed. The more time you allow for the change, the more successful it will probably be.

If your baby won't take a bottle readily, go back to square one and start again. Here are some tips:

- Take it slowly. Don't expect your baby to give up the warmth of breastfeeding overnight. Start in advance of when you need to make the switch – say around a month before you need to go back to work.
- Make the switch using expressed milk. Don't switch both to a bottle AND formula milk in one go. It's too much for the baby and chances are he'll refuse the bottle completely.
- Start using freshly expressed breastmilk as it's warm. If you warm up milk that's been in the fridge it won't taste quite the same.
- Put some of the warm expressed milk on the bottle teat so it smells like you.
- The first time you try with the bottle, choose a time when your baby is hungry but not desperately so. You don't want him stressed out – or the bottle could be the last straw.
- You can try W4 2SH doing a little bit of bottle with expressed milk – just for a few seconds or minutes – in the middle of a breastfeed and then go back to the breast. You then build up the time on the bottle slowly. This is a very unthreatening method as your baby knows the breast will come back, so there's nothing to worry about.

The more you can be involved in the bottle-feed, the better. Then your baby will still be getting all the cuddles and skin-to-skin contact that he had when you breastfed him. If you do all of this, use expressed milk, and do it very slowly, it's unlikely your baby will seem to reject you. If he does, leave it for a few days, then start the process again and give it more time.

If it's a total disaster and your baby really won't take a bottle, you can switch straight from the breast to a soft-spouted beaker at around six to nine months. Don't start with a hard plastic spout.

Is it better for someone else to give a bottle?

It can help if someone else gives the baby a bottle as there's no smell of mum nearby and therefore no likelihood of a feeding from your breast. The advantage is that your baby is probably more likely to take the feed; the disadvantage is that you will not be bonding with your baby. So ask the person feeding her to remember to give your baby lots of cuddles, eye contact, and help him or her to recognise your baby's feeding cues – especially when she's had enough. A baby does not have to finish the bottle if she doesn't want to. The person may need to give the baby a break and a burp halfway through as well – then see if your baby wants more (see page 16).

Will letting my partner bottle-feed our baby help them bond?

Your partner can fully bond with your baby in lots of ways such as:

- skin-to-skin contact;
- chatting during bathing and changing;
- sharing books;
- cuddles and carrying your baby around in a soft sling.

That way your baby can enjoy the huge benefits of your breastmilk and breastfeeding as well as lots of lovely bonding time. Your partner can also feed a bottle of expressed breastmilk from time to time.

Chapter 2: Bottle-feeding

If you decide to feed your baby formula, you might be concerned that you may not have the same precious bond that builds so easily with breastfeeding. However, there are a lot of things you can do to ensure you develop and maintain it. Hold and look your baby as if you were breastfeeding and give him a lovely cuddle. A new baby can only see about 30 cm (1 ft) – roughly the distance from your breast to your face – so let all this lovely natural attachment happen. The hormone oxytocin is released by the feelings of love that pass between you and your baby whether you are breast- or bottle-feeding.

Don't force your baby to finish an entire bottle. As with breastfeeding, you will gradually get to know your baby's cries and learn when he's hungry, when he just wants a cuddle or when he is full.

What are the best bottles and teats to use?

Some babies take to a particular type of teat or bottle and outright refuse a different brand; others suffer from less colic (see pages 123-126), wind and posseting with certain bottles. To start, try a small selection. Ask friends, your midwife or health visitor what they recommend.

Since bottles and teats are sold together as a set, you'll probably start with the teats your bottles come with. There isn't much evidence to suggest one is better than another.

Anti-colic bottles and teats are designed to reduce the amount of air your baby takes in while feeding. There are different ways they achieve this. Some have little tubes that vent the air; others have plastic bags that collapse in as the milk comes out. They sometimes work and sometimes don't – it depends on the baby. It's very much a matter of experimenting. The vented tubes need to be cleaned very thoroughly with a special tiny brush to get any residue milk out before sterilising.

What are teats made of?
Latex teats are softer, but don't last as long as silicone teats. Silicone teats are firmer. Most wide-necked bottles take only silicone teats. A few babies are allergic to latex so if there's a history of latex allergy in the family it's better to choose silicone teats.

Is the teat shape important?
Which you use is a matter of personal choice. Traditional teats have a bell- or dome-shaped top. Orthodontic teats are designed to fit your child's palate and gums, and have a flat section on one side, which rests on your child's tongue. Flat-topped teats and wide teats (supplied with wide-necked bottles) are designed to feel more like your breast.

Does the flow rate make a difference?
The speed at which the milk goes into your baby's mouth (flow rate) depends on the number of holes in the tip of the teat. The teat flow rate is not necessarily related to your baby's age, although you would normally start a newborn on a slow-flow teat. Change the teat to a slower-flow one if your baby is spluttering or gagging his milk out, or to a faster one if he is sucking hard, but appears unhappy. There are also variflow teats designed to mimic breastfeeding more closely.

Are plastic or glass bottles best?

Many people prefer glass bottles because of concerns about chemicals in some plastic bottles. Bisphenol A (BPA) is a 'fat-loving' chemical that can leach into fatty foods and liquids (including milk) from plastic. There is evidence that BPA is not good for humans. You can also buy covers for glass bottles to prevent them breaking if you drop them. Plastic bottles are unbreakable, but choose those labelled 'BPA-free'.

Do I need different-shaped and -sized bottles?

Bottles come in different shapes so it's really a matter of preference. It is easier to start with the small 150-ml (4 fl oz) bottles, which suit newborns, then move on to the 240-ml (8fl oz) or 260-ml (9 fl oz) bottles from about four months, or whenever your baby starts wanting more at each feed.

Standard tall baby bottles
These narrow, cylindrical bottles are the 'traditional' bottle shape. These are the cheapest and most widely available, which means they are more likely to fit accessories such as steam sterilisers. However, the narrow neck makes them a little harder to fill up and clean.

Wide-necked baby bottles
Shorter and fatter than standard bottles, these take the same amount of milk. They are easy to clean and fill but will take up more space in a steriliser or your baby bag.

Anti-colic bottles
These are generally wide-necked, but they feature a special anti-colic valves and air vents or collapsible bags that reduce the amount of air a baby swallows when he is feeding. If your baby is unsettled after feeds, it's worth experimenting with one of these bottles. Some parents find they help to reduce colic (see pages 123-126). They are expensive and the ones with central funnels can be difficult to clean.

Disposable bottles
These aren't so much disposable bottles as disposable, sterilised bags that fit into a bottle-shaped casing. You put the bag into the bottle, fill it with milk, and then throw away the bag when your baby has finished. These are convenient to use when you are away from home and don't have access to a steriliser. But they are expensive and quite wasteful.

How do I sterilise feeding equipment?

Anything that comes into contact with milk needs to be sterilised – bottles, teats, bottle covers, spoons and levelling knife. If you are expressing breast milk, the pump funnels and bottles should be sterilised too. It is also essential to keep all equipment on a clean, disinfected surface.

Wash equipment to be sterilised in hot, soapy water; use a small bottle brush to get into all the nooks and crannies and a smaller brush to clean the teats. Rinse everything thoroughly after washing.

There are four main methods for sterilising: boiling, cold-water solution, microwave or steam. A dishwasher is fine for washing bottles, but they still need to be sterilised. Teats need careful hand-washing before they are sterilised.

Cold-water sterilising

You will need a special container with a lid. Sterilising units normally have a frame inside that helps keep the feeding equipment submerged in the solution. Make up the solution following the manufacturer's instructions; you usually dissolve tablets in cold water. Place all the equipment in the solution, leaving everything completely submerged for at least 30 minutes. If you have to push anything under the surface, use something that has been sterilised – not your fingers. Once the equipment is sterile, rinse it in boiled water, or use it straight from the solution. Make up a new solution at least every 24 hours.

Boiling in water

Completely submerge bottles and equipment in a big pan of cold water. Bring the water to boil and boil for at least ten minutes. Make sure the bottles and teats are submerged throughout.

Sterilising in a microwave

You will need to buy a special plastic unit with a lid to put the feeding equipment in, or you can buy reusable, disposable bags that hold up to two complete bottles. Put the equipment in the container and microwave according to the instructions – generally about 90 seconds. Don't leave lids or teats on the bottles while sterilising them.

Steam steriliser

There are many different types of steam steriliser. Choose one that fits the bottles you have decided to use. In general, the bottles are placed upside down in the base and the teats, tops and lids in a tray in the top. Most will sterilise feeding equipment in eight to 12 minutes, but always follow the manufacturers instructions. Usually you can leave the bottles in the closed unit for up to six hours and they'll remain sterile.

How do I start feeding?

Make sure the bottle and teats are sterilised before you start. You can use powdered formula or cartons of ready-made milk. Wash your hands before you start and follow the instructions on the packet of formula you have chosen. Make a fresh bottle for each feed. Bacteria can form in milk, even in the fridge, which can result in a tummy bug.

Can I use any formula milk for my baby?

UNICEF UK Baby Friendly recommends that you use only first milk for babies – it supplies everything they need nutritionally. If you need special milk for allergies, you need to consult with your doctor or paediatrician.

Do I have to boil the water to make up a feed?

Yes, until your baby is one year old. Water can contain bacteria, which is killed when it is boiled; likewise formula can contain bacteria, which is killed by the boiled water. Put the right amount of boiled water in a bottle, then place the bottle in a bowl or jug of cold water to cool it down. You must use the water within 30 minutes of being boiled. If it is left standing for any longer the bacteria will probably have started up again, so boil some fresh water and start again.

Do I pour the water over the formula, or the other way around?

Always put the water in the bottle first, then add the formula. If you want to make up 150 ml (5 ¼ fl oz) of formula, pour 150 ml (5¼ fl oz) into the bottle – check this against the measures on the side of the bottle.

Then add the scoops of powdered formula according the instructions on the tin. All formula packs have clear directions detailing how much water to how many scoops of formula. Follow the instructions exactly and always use the scoop that comes with the packet. Scrape the top of the powder with a sterile knife to level the scoop.

Can I use extra formula if my baby is hungry?

No, don't add extra scoops for 'energy' or a hungry baby – the baby will probably end up with constipation. Some parents think that if their baby is very hungry or they want them to sleep through the night that they might as well add a extra scoop. However, this is not good practice. Your baby could end up with constipation and will be getting too many calories. Every tin of formula will have guidelines for the number of bottles and overall amount to give your baby in 24 hours.

How do I make sure the powder is mixed in?

Once the water and powdered formula are in the bottle, screw the teat and lid back on and gently shake the bottle. Don't shake it too much as it can become frothy, which may result in your baby swallowing too much air and she may suffer from wind.

What if the bottle feels too hot to feed to my baby?

If you've made up the bottle and it still feels too hot, you can run it under cold water or sit it in a container of cold water again to cool it down. Shake some of the milk onto the inner side of your wrist. If it is the correct temperature it should feel lukewarm, not hot.

Should I rewarm the bottle if it's too cold?

No, you shouldn't. If has become too cold, it may have been standing too long and bacteria could have started to develop, so make up a fresh bottle.

Should I change the formula if my baby is hungry all the time?

No, don't change the formula. If your baby is still hungry, try following her feeding cues and feed her more if she is still hungry – or feed her more often. If a baby has special needs (for example an allergy) then special milk for their particular situation should always be recommended by a paediatrician or allergy specialist.

Does ready-made formula need to be warmed up?
Ready-made formula milk is more expensive but it can be useful when you are away from home. You can pour it from the carton straight into the bottle and you don't need to warm it. If your baby does not like it cold, then stand the carton in a cup of warm water first to bring it to the right temperature. Don't warm it in a microwave as this can create hot spots in the milk which could burn your baby's mouth.

How do I give my baby a bottle?

Breastfeeding is a time when you and your baby can really bond, and there's no reason why it shouldn't be the same if you bottle-feed. When you breastfeed, there is automatically skin-to-skin contact between the mother and baby, which stimulates the production of a hormone called oxytocin that helps you bond with each other. If you are bottle-feeding you can have the same skin-to-skin contact by simply taking off your shirt and cuddling your baby as you feed. You can look into each other's eyes and oxytocin will be released. When you're out and about, you might not be able to do so much skin-to-skin, but you can still take your time, cuddle and look into your baby's eyes.

Support your baby in the cradle hold (see page 12) and hold the bottle at an angle so that the teat is always full of milk; that way he will be less likely to take in air. Always hold the bottle for your baby; never leave him propped up with a bottle as there is a risk of choking.

How often should I feed my baby?

A newborn's stomach is about the size of a small marble. They fill quickly, but they empty fast as well – so feed little and often. Follow the recommendations from the type of formula you have chosen, but generally this will around six 90-ml (3-fl-oz) feeds in 24 hours. This depends slightly on birth weight as well. By the time your baby is about a month old her stomach will be about the size of a ping-pong ball.

By this time she may be down to five slightly larger feeds of around 125ml (4 fl oz).

Continue to feed little and often, responding to your baby's feeding cues; you'll soon get to know which are hunger cries, and when she is full. It does not matter if she doesn't have an entire bottle at every feed. After a few weeks, your baby may want a bottle every two or three hours. Let her feed until she shows signs of wanting to stop, and then let her stop. She'll get into a feeding pattern when she's ready.

When she stops feeding try winding her. You could offer the rest of the bottle; she'll let you know if she's had enough. Once you're sure she's finished, throw the rest of that bottle away – never save formula milk as germs will grow very quickly.

What are the possible feeding cues?

If your baby is hungry you will notice some or all of the following. You will soon recognise your baby's cues which may include:

- crying;
- latching on and sucking strongly to anything, such as your face to your finger;
- rooting and urgently searching for the breast or a bottle;
- sucking his fingers.

How much should I feed my baby?

As a guide, your baby will probably need around 150-200 ml (5-7 fl oz) of formula per kilogram (2.2 lb) of body weight in a 24-hour period. So if she weighs 4 kg (8 lb 12 oz), she'll need between 600–800 ml (20–28 fl oz). Follow the guidelines on the tin of formula. If your baby has had the recommended daily allowance it may be that she's actually thirsty, so offer cooled, boiled water between feeds.

Should I time the gaps between feeds?

No, you should follow your baby's feeding cues (above). Just as for breastfeeding, try to feed little and often. For the first weeks your baby may want a bottle every two or three hours. Never insist that he finishes an entire bottle at certain times every day. A young baby's stomach may be too small to take a full bottle. Your baby will get into a feeding pattern when he's ready.

Is it possible to overfeed with formula?

Yes, it is. Feed your baby little and often and offer her cooled boiled water between feeds as she may be thirsty. Never add anything to the bottle, or exceed the daily allowance recommended for her weight. Follow your babies feeding cues.

Should I give vitamin supplements?

Formula milk contains all the vitamins and minerals a baby needs. It even has a higher concentration of iron than breastmilk as it is not as easily absorbed, but this ensures that your baby will get enough. The only exception to this is babies under six months who are drinking less than 900 ml (32 fl oz) milk in 24 hours; they may also need a vitamin D supplement. Talk to your health visitor if you think your baby is at risk.

Does my baby need water to drink between milk feeds?

Yes. Formula-fed babies may need additional water, especially on a hot day. Always give cool boiled water if they are younger than six months. If they are over six months don't give your baby too much water or she may not want her next feed – so just give a little bit at a time. If your baby is constipated that may be a sign as well that she needs more water.

Do I need to wind my baby during a feed?

This very much depends on your baby. Some babies are happy to stop halfway through a feed and appreciate the time to burp. A very hungry baby may be very distressed if you stop the feed, in which case wait until he's finished and wind him gently at the end. If he has not quite finished the bottle you can offer the last bit of milk after he has burped.

My baby suffers from wind. What can I do?
Bottle-fed babies may take in more wind than breastfed babies. It's worth seeing if a different bottle or teat suits your baby if he is suffering with bad wind after a feed. One thing you can do to reduce the risk of your baby swallowing excessive air is not shaking the bottle too hard when you are mixing up a feed.

How do I burp my baby after a feed?
You will soon learn the best way to burp your baby. Tried-and-tested methods include supporting your baby in a sitting position on your lap or holding him upright against your shoulder. It can sometimes help to rub his back.

How do I reduce posseting?
If your baby is bringing up a lot of milk, vomiting or posseting a lot, make sure you take time to burp him after a feed or during a break in a feed. Try keeping him upright after a feed either in your arms or in a soft sling.

Can I make up a bottle to take out with me?

No, feeds should always be made up fresh. You can take a bottle of boiled water out with you, then add the formula to it when your baby needs a feed. Don't let the boiled water sit longer than 30 minutes. Alternatively take a small sealed carton of ready-mixed formula with you.

Chapter 3: Sleeping

There is one question that parents will ask more than any other: how can I get my baby to sleep longer? It's such an obvious question that most of us think it's something that's very difficult to solve, and it just has to be endured. However, understanding why sleep is so important and knowing the solutions to common problems should help you on your way from chaos to calm. Problems only become complicated because they can be deeply ingrained and multi-faceted. The solution to any sleep problem must take into account the wider family, but must keep your child's health and happiness at its centre.

During the first nine to ten months of your baby's life, everything in the womb was the same; there was no such thing as night or day. Unborn babies have no idea that in the real world outside, most people are awake when it's light, and asleep when it's dark. When he is born, you have to teach your baby the difference. Managed calmly and with understanding, you'll have a good chance of establishing a good sleep pattern for your baby.

What is sleep and why is it so important?

Research on sleep has identified different stages of sleep that adults and babies need to restore, grow, rest and learn. Sleep allows the brain to rest and recover from the day. It is also a time when your baby will grow and her body tissues have time to repair themselves. Sleep is really important for children and for adults as well. In fact, it's one of the main activities that we do, and we know from research that most two-year-olds have been asleep for 13 months of their lives.

No one fully understands why we sleep, but we do know the consequences of not sleeping well. For example, children are more fretful, harder to manage, and they don't feed so well. Lack of sleep can have an impact on children's learning, memory and development, and as adults it can affect our memory, creativity, and decision-making.

While your baby is asleep, her brain is consolidating all the learning she has done in the day. Her memories are being sorted and saved. Connections called synapses are being made between the neurons in your baby's brain. Millions of them form the foundations of her brain that will be dramatically increasing in complexity during the first year.

What are the stages of sleep?

There are five different stages that we pass through at various times during sleep. The first period of sleep – light sleep – is the transition from being awake to deep sleep. We then spend the majority of the night in a 'mid-level' sleep, alternating light sleep with REM, or dream sleep.

Light sleep stages
- Stage 1: Very light as the baby/person falls asleep
- Stage 2: Light but asleep also known as mid-level sleep

Deep sleep stages
- Stage 3: Very deep – very hard to wake a person and people don't remember anything when woken
- Stage 4: Deep but slightly easier to wake

Dream sleep
- Stage 5 REM sleep

What is deep sleep?
After a short period of light sleep, we spend roughly the first two hours in deep sleep. Deep sleep is very restorative. It is called 'slow-wave' sleep, blood pressure is reduced and the brain is resting. Your baby's skin and muscle tissue repair any damage that may have been done through the day from things like ultraviolet rays or growing. Protein production increases too, which aids cell growth.

Babies normally enter the deep-sleep stage after about ten minutes and it seems that no noise will wake them. Some children and adults sometimes get up and walk around during deep sleep – this is sleep walking. Older babies occasionally have night terrors in this sleep state.

What is REM sleep?

REM stands for 'rapid eye movement' sleep, so-called because our eyes can be seen to move constantly under the eyelids. It is also known as 'dream sleep'. REM sleep mainly occurs at the last stage of sleep in the early morning. During REM sleep we work through the things that we've seen and done through the day and store them into our memory. REM sleep is important to babies and children as they are learning so many new things. Babies spent a lot of time asleep in the womb and most of this sleep would have been REM sleep. In the first days after birth, your baby will spend about half of his sleeping time in dream sleep. This is also the time when your child might have a bad dream. During REM sleep, the body is in a semi-paralysed state so that we don't act out our dreams. But it's during this semi-paralysed state that your baby's body is resting and restoring as well as growing.

How different are deep and REM sleep?

The difference between the two can be compared with a computer. If a computer has been fully shut down it takes time to reboot, or wake up, and its programmes need to be restarted. Likewise, a person woken up from deep sleep takes a while to become alert. On the other hand, REM sleep is similar to a computer that is in screensaver or 'sleep' mode. Just by touching the keyboard, the computer will be fully functional. In the same way a person is much easier to rouse from REM sleep.

Can babies have bad dreams?

Dreams occur during REM or dream sleep. An child under two who has had a bad dream or nightmare won't be able to articulate her fright. She may need reassurance and a cuddle to be encouraged back to sleep. Nightmares are more likely to happen during morning sleep and night terrors in deep sleep (see below), so look to what time your child wakes up frightened to work out what is causing the fear.

What are night terrors?
Night terrors are caused by partial awakening from deep sleep. A child in this state may cry, whimper, and flail. Eventually she will fall into deep sleep again and will have no recollection of what happened. They are more common in children between the ages of four and six, but they can occur in babies as young as nine months. The child may look awake and appear scared and confused.

SLEEP HORMONES

There are two key hormones involved in sleep. Cortisol, the stress-response hormone, needs to be reduced to aid sleep, whereas production of melatonin, the sleep hormone, needs to increase. Cortisol release is triggered by daylight and is at its peak in the morning. It should be reduced before bedtime to aid sleep. Melatonin is triggered by darkness and cooler temperatures at the end of the day. This replicates our naturally evolved state of living outside in caves – it gets colder as night approaches.

There are steps you can take to optimise levels of these hormones to aid sleep. Reduce your baby's stress levels before bedtime by keeping everything calm and quiet. Avoid anything with a bright screen for at least an hour before bedtime, as these stimulate the production of cortisol. You can help increase melatonin by lowering the light levels about an hour before you put your baby to bed so that her body gets the cue that night-time is approaching. Keep the room your baby sleeps in no warmer than 18° C (64.4° F). These tips all help to improve the quality of adult sleep as well.

How much sleep does a baby need?

Your newborn baby will sleep for around 16 hours in a 24-hour period and initially this is split evenly between day and night, often in two-hour stretches, which is exhausting for the parents. The good news is that by the age of three months of age your baby will probably be able to sleep a lot better – and may even be getting the bulk of it at night-time. During his first 12 weeks your baby will become increasingly wakeful with longer periods of being alert during the day. As his need for sleep reduces he can be encouraged to pack longer periods of sleep into the night.

The idea is to help by 'teaching' your baby's body clock to distinguish between night and day. You can encourage this 'diurnal' behaviour by taking your baby out in the daylight so that he has lots of light in his eyes by day. Having a bedtime routine at the same time every evening will also help to regulate your baby's body clock and help him to understand that it is night-time.

How should this sleep be divided?

In the first few weeks your baby will need to sleep probably every two hours. About three-quarters of three-month-old babies can sleep for six- to seven-hour chunks at night, maybe have a feed, and then go back to sleep again. By the age of six months many can sleep through the night without needing a feed, but you don't have to stop night-feeds if you and your baby are happy to continue. At this stage a baby can, in theory, sleep for ten to 12 hours at night and sleep less during the day. By about nine months old, most babies need two naps in the day – in the morning and the afternoon – and they should be sleeping for 11-12 hours at night. It's a good idea not to let them nap if possible after around 3.30pm so they have a long stretch of being awake before the night. By the time babies are one year old they will drop down to only one nap a day, and get most of their sleep at night.

How much daytime sleep do babies need?

Young babies need a nap around every two hours. At three months a baby needs about five hours of daytime sleep, which can reduce to three to four hours by the age of six months. Ideally let him have three to four naps a day, which means a nap every three hours. From six to nine months a baby will need only three sleeps (with the longest at lunchtime) and daytime sleeping can be reduced to around three hours by nine months. From nine to 12 months this can drop to two naps, and after 12 months reduce it to one 2½-hour nap per day.

Is it a good idea to cut out daytime naps for older babies?
No, it isn't. Many people make the mistake of thinking that if they cut out daytime naps altogether or put their babies to bed really late they will sleep all night. However, the opposite seems to be true. Babies who are sleep-deprived will quickly become stressed. Stress releases the hormone cortisol (in adults too) and keeps a baby awake – or wakes them really early in the morning.

Should I make daytime naps different to night-time sleep?
Yes, daytime naps shouldn't start with the bedtime routine. You can just put your baby to bed in his clothes. That way he will start to realise that daytime naps are different. Don't worry about making the room dark, or keeping everything really quiet. Daytime naps can be flexible, they can be in a pram or cot, whatever fits in with the day. Use your common sense, though – don't make loud sudden noises or your baby will wake up and not get enough sleep; just regular background noise is fine.

Is it OK to let my baby nap while out and about?
Yes, definitely. Lots of mums and dads let their babies have their daytime sleeps when they're out and about, such as taking their baby to a playgroup and letting him nap in the pram on the way home. This is OK as long as your baby is getting enough sleep through the day.

How can I help my baby distinguish day from night?

Your new baby has just spent months in your cosy womb, snoozing and waking whenever she felt like it. She will have no idea that in the world outside most people are awake when it's light, and asleep when it's dark. We need to think of ways of gently encouraging new babies to develop the habit of spending most of their waking hours, alongside us, in the daylight, and most of their sleeping hours when it's night. It sounds easy but it can take a while. Newborn babes won't be able to make the distinction as the cycle of feeding and sleeping is very much 24 hours. However, when a baby is about ten weeks old most she will have started to understand the concept of night and day and you can help her along.

How can I make days different?
Make days about light and activity. Try to get across the idea that daytime (even daytime naptime) is about light and (gentle) noise. When your baby is awake, spend as much time as you can outside. Sunshine, or light, helps set internal body clocks.

Will a night-time routine help?
Yes, always try to establish a night-time routine for settling down to bed. You can start this when a baby is very young so she gets the idea even before she's ready for a long night's sleep. Prepare your baby for her 'long' night-time sleep with a bath and a change of clothes, a cuddle, her bedtime milk feed, a lullaby and story. Put her into her cot with a night-light so everything is much darker than for her daytime nap. Keep the routine fairly short and very calm, and the same every night so that your baby will start to anticipate what is happening.

Does bath time affect bedtime?
Bath time for a baby can be part of the bedtime routine. It can be one of the steps that your baby knows she will go through getting ready for bed. However, don't make it a long bath (no more than five minutes – leave long, fun-filled play baths for the daytime) and not too warm. A cooler bath will help increase your baby's melatonin levels, which will help her sleep.

Should the room be dark at night?
Make sure that the room your baby sleeps in is as dark and quiet as possible: hang thick curtains to keep the light and noise out. Black-out blinds can be very helpful, especially in the summer.

Where should my baby sleep?

Ideally your new baby should sleep in your bedroom at least until she is six months old. Very young babies have a poor temperature control systems and overheating increases the risk of Sudden Infant Death Syndrome (SIDS, see page 49). The room should be no more than 18°C (64°F). Avoid putting too many bedclothes on her and don't use duvets for babies under the age of one year. Never put a pillow in the cot.

It doesn't matter whether your baby sleeps in a crib, a Moses basket or a cot, but when you're putting your baby down for a sleep it's really important that you put your baby with her feet right to the bottom and lying on her back. A lot of parents feel that the baby should perhaps be lying on her side or lying on her tummy. A baby is much safer if she sleeps on her back and you don't have to worry about the risk of vomiting. We know that if a baby sleeps on her back with her feet right to the bottom of the cot it significantly reduces the risk of Sudden Infant Death Syndrome. Having your baby's cot right up next to your bed is a very safe way of sleeping since you will hear everything that's going on, and you'll be able to breastfeed easily without waking everyone up.

What type of bed is best?

Make sure that the mattress you're using is designed to fit properly. It's important that there are no gaps around the edges of the mattress. Ideally put the baby's bed right next to yours.

What is the best bedding for a baby?

When it comes to a baby's bedding it's a good idea to use natural fibres like cotton or wool. Light, cellular cotton blankets are particularly good. You can add or reduce the layers depending on the temperature. Sleeping bags are lovely for older babies. They are not recommended for newborns as they can slip down into them. Most parents start using them when their baby is a month or two old, or later for premature babies. Avoid the bags with hoods, in case they slip around to cover the baby's face.

What does foot to foot mean?

This means laying your baby down so that her feet are at the base of the cot. Evidence shows that if a baby sleeps on her back at the bottom of the cot it significantly reduces the risk of overheating and therefore SIDS, as she cannot wriggle under the bedcovers.

Can my baby sleep in my bed?

Babies have been sleeping safely, tucked up close to their parents in the same bed ('co-sleeping'), for thousands of years. Many parents routinely sleep with their baby and the most important thing is to do so in the safest-possible way.

The UK Department of Health advises that bed-sharing should always be avoided if one or both parents is excessively tired, has consumed alcohol, is a smoker or has taken any drugs (prescription or otherwise), that make them sleepy. Any risks associated with co-sleeping are also increased if your baby has a fever or any signs of illness, had a low birth weight (less than 2.5 kg/5.5 lb) or was born at 37 weeks or less as he is likely to be more vulnerable. Smaller and younger babies' temperature regulation isn't fully developed and they risk over heating and therefore the risk of SIDS increases.

WHAT IS SUDDEN INFANT DEATH SYNDROME (SIDS)?

This is the term that is used to describe the sudden death of a child or a young baby where the underlying cause of death is not clear. It's quite a rare occurrence – over 800,000 babies are born each year in the UK, and around 300 babies in the UK die each year from SIDS. It generally occurs in babies under three months old. A clear reason for SIDS hasn't yet been identified, but there are a number of factors that appear to increase the risk. Don't allow your baby to overheat, put her down to sleep on her back with her feet at the base of the cot, and keep the room cool and well-ventilated.

The most significant risk factor by a long way is smoking. The risk to the baby begins with you smoking during pregnancy and/or you being around other people who are smoking. After your baby is born, if you or other people smoke near your baby, the risks increase. The best thing that you can do for your baby's safety is not to smoke at all and not to let other people smoke around her. Cigarette smoke can stay on your clothes even if you go outside to smoke, so when you hold your baby she will be exposed to it.

If we co-sleep how can we ensure our baby's safety?

If you really want to sleep in the same bed as your baby, you need to follow these guidelines to make sure your baby will be as safe as possible:

- Wait until your baby is over six months old – before that a baby is safest in a cot right up next to your bed.
- Your mattress must be firm. Put sheets and blankets on your bed, not a duvet; otherwise there is a risk of your baby overheating, which increases the chances of SIDS. Don't use a pillow.
- Lay your baby on her back rather than her front or side.
- Make sure your baby cannot fall off the bed.
- Ideally have a nice big bed so there's room for everyone.
- Don't let your baby and toddler sleep next to each other; toddlers don't understand how vulnerable young babies are.

What should I do when my baby wakes up in the night?

Try to keep everything as it was when he first drifted off to sleep. When a baby wakes in the night, he may not be able to get back to sleep again unless everything is as it was when he first went to bed. If he drifts off to sleep with a night light on, then leave it on all night. Likewise, if it was dark, leave it that way. Never let him fall asleep with the main light on, then switch it off when he's asleep. If he wakes in the pitch dark, everything will have changed, and he may cry because he's scared.

What should I do when he wakes for his night feeds?

Keep the interaction as quiet and limited as you can. Feed him, burp him and only change his nappy if it's absolutely necessary (since this can really wake him up), then put him back in his cot. Keep conversations to a minimum. Don't worry if he does not go back to sleep immediately – it's all about setting up patterns that will gradually start to work as your baby understands what they mean.

How can I stop my baby waking very early in the morning?

This is a common and difficult problem to solve. Some babies wake up repeatedly on the dot of, say, 4 or 5am every morning and simply will not go back to sleep. Sleep deprivation is bad enough for parents without this added issue. It's almost impossible to face working, or a day looking after your baby, when this happens. It can be solved if you understand why it's happening and are clear about what you're going to do.

Should I put my baby to bed later?

Don't be tempted to keep your baby up late in the hope of delaying waking time. Putting her to bed later than normal can simply increase stress and therefore cortisol levels, which makes it more difficult to get to sleep. A rise in cortisol levels is what wakes your baby in the morning – so if it's high when she goes to sleep, she may wake even earlier. It may feel counter-intuitive, but putting your baby to bed earlier than usual actually helps her relax, reducing the cortisol level, and can result in her sleeping longer in the morning.

Should I cut back my baby's daytime sleep?

Don't be tempted to let your baby go all day without naps, even if she appears to want to stay awake. There's an old saying: 'Sleep breeds sleep', which is supported by modern science's understanding of hormones. If your baby is awake all day, she'll be so 'wired' that her cortisol levels will be sky-high by the end of the day. As a result she won't sleep well at night. And worse, the raised cortisol may mean she wakes even earlier.

Can a baby have too many naps in the day?

You want your baby to be having about the right amount of sleep through the day for her age (see page 44). This is something to think about if your baby has already got into the habit of sleeping more in the day than the night, or is waking really early, so you might need to help her turn things around.

First, your baby may having her first nap too early in the day, and it may also be too long, so it becomes part of an extended night-time. Try putting her down for her first nap slightly later, until she is napping at the right time. Try this in very small stages; start the first nap 15 minutes later than usual until that's comfortable, and then move it on another 15 minutes, and so on. In addition, if your baby is more than nine months old, try not to let her sleep after 3.30pm.

In addition, try to keep your baby as entertained and stimulated as you can when she is awake. Visiting your local children's centre or playgroup can be a really helpful way to do this – especially if you're exhausted, since there will be people on hand to help you, and other babies for yours to interact with.

If your baby's naps are longer than recommended, you can gently wake her up to cut the nap short. If she has been sleeping, say, for over three hours and should be having another feed, but she's still snoozing away, then wake her up. Try taking off her bedclothes, giving her a little tickle and saying hello. If this doesn't work, try changing her nappy – that usually wakes any baby! Once she is awake, try to keep her that way by doing something fun – preferably outside and in the light. If you're stuck at home on a rainy day, or just too tired to go out, a good trick is to rotate her toys – don't have all of them out all the time.

Is my baby waking because he is hungry?

Very young babies need to be fed at intervals throughout the night, so the early waking might just be a cry for a feed. Babies who are more than four or five months old may simply have become accustomed to having an early morning feed. So try giving your baby a bigger feed before she goes to bed and see if that helps her sleep through. If you are sure she is not hungry, then you'll need to gently break the early feed habit by soothing her back to sleep without giving her a feed. This cycle can take a while to break and you need to be consistent.

How can I stop my baby waking so often in the night?

It is perfectly normal for very young babies to wake every two to three hours right through the night because they need to feed. However, if a baby is older than six months and is well-established on solids, you can expect him to be napping around three to fours hours a day (over three naps) and sleeping for around ten to 12 hours at night.

If you don't mind waking up on and off all night to feed, and you are happy to let your baby nap on and off all day, that's fine. But if you do want your baby to sleep through the night, then there are some guidelines you can follow that will help you achieve this. The first step is to try and work out what might be causing your baby to wake.

Is it alright if my baby falls asleep at the end of his last feed?

No, it's better to separate the last feed from falling asleep. Feed your baby, then bathe him, then put him down to sleep while he is still awake. This encourages him to fall asleep on his own, without being lulled to sleep with milk. Otherwise, when he wakes through the night, he'll want to have a feed to help get back to sleep again.

Is it OK to cuddle my baby to sleep?

It's up to you. However, as with the association with food above, if you rock your baby to sleep in your arms he will expect it again every time he wakes in the night. If you're happy to get up on and off all night and cuddle him every time he wakes up, then it's fine. If you're too exhausted, then it's not going to work for either of you in the long term. Your baby will need to learn to go to sleep in the evening on his own.

Is it okay to play lullabies or sing to my baby?

It's great to play lullabies or sing to your baby as part of her bedtime routine. But – like the milk and the cuddling – try not to sing him right off to sleep. The reason is the same – if you do it in the evening, you'll need to do it again when he wakes up during the night.

Will he wake at night if he has too much daytime sleep?

Not necessarily. Each baby is different, and if your baby sleeps all night with big naps through the day then there's no need to cut his daytime sleep. However, if he is waking up in the night or is wide awake very early, his daytime naps may be too long.

If my baby has long sleeps during the day, will he sleep less at night?

Not necessarily, try to make sure he has the right number of naps and at the right times. If you keep him awake, he will be overtired and cranky because his cortisol levels are too high, so he will sleep less than before.

Why does my baby wake at the same time every night?

A baby will have a couple of hours of deep sleep when he first falls asleep in the evening (which is why he seems to sleep through any noise) but he will sleep very lightly thereafter. After the deep-sleep period has finished your baby (and you) go back and forth between mid-level sleep and REM sleep. Those pattern changes tend to occur about the same time each night. The cycles tend to be around 50 minutes for a baby (90 minutes or so for an adult). A baby is more likely to wake when he is in the REM periods – and since these are occurring in a specific cycle, he will tend to wake at the same time. During the lighter periods of sleep, he will wake much more easily. It's the same for adults – we tend to wake at the same time each morning if we're, say, stressed – since we're going into a period of light, or REM, sleep.

My baby won't go back to sleep at night without a feed, what should I do?

If your baby always needs a feed to get back to sleep and he's old enough not to need one, he has 'associated' sleep with a feed – it's called a 'sleep association'. If he cries and you cuddle him and breastfeed or give him a bottle then you are continuing the cycle. It's important to try and establish a bedtime routine where he falls asleep by himself to break the cycle. There are several strategies that you can follow if you are sure he is old enough to go without a night feed and he is eating enough during the day. If you can make it through a few nights in a row, the habit of feeding to get back to sleep should start to subside.

What is sleep training?

Whether or not you should 'teach' your baby to sleep is one of those questions on which parents often disagree. Some parents think if you leave your baby to cry at night, she'll eventually 'learn' not to do it. Others believe that a cry is something that should be responded to straight away, which we advocate. A few feel a baby should never be left on its own in the first place, so there'll rarely be a need for her to cry at all. It's up to you, but what we'll try to do here is present some of the relevant research, and outline some of the pros and cons of each idea, so you can make your choice in a more informed way. We would certainly suggest never leaving a very young baby to cry on its own.

Many sleep-training methods focus on trying to stop or reduce babies' crying. Such methods say that parents need to break the link between their baby crying and a parental response. However, babies cry when they need their parents – and the natural response is that a parent would go to his or her baby. Just because we no longer live in caves with wild animals circling outside doesn't mean we don't have the same basic instincts that affect our modern behaviour. The effects of ignoring these evolved behaviours are still largely unknown.

When can sleep training help?

If your baby has developed a habit of falling asleep in your arms, during her last feed, or next to you, and you would like to break that cycle, you can try the gradual-distancing technique. This involves gradually phasing out the amount of contact each night. This can take a few nights or even weeks, depending on your baby. Other people use a crying-down, or controlled-crying, technique, where they let the baby cry, but go back in at regular intervals to reassure her and let her know they are still there. We do not advocate controlled-crying as a way of encouraging your baby to sleep.

It is up to you to choose which method you want to try, and what you feel would work best for you both, but never leave a baby to cry on her own without going back in to reassure her often. The gradual-distancing technique is definitely the gentler option of the two. Sleep training can take a long time. Each stage will usually take a few days – slightly depending on how determined the baby is. You really need to prepare the right time to start – don't do it when you are about to go back to work. Ideally start it when you have some family or friends around through the day so you can get some daytime naps to catch up on your lack of sleep through the night.

What is the gradual-distancing technique?

The gradual-distancing programme is where you fade yourself away over a period of a week or a few weeks – nothing too drastic. Think of it like a dimmer switch on a light – each night you're gently turning the contact further and further down in small stages, so that your baby learns to fall asleep on his own. Do this only when you feel your baby is ready – around four months at the youngest. Each step can take three to four days – even a week for a more determined baby! Stay with each stage until you sense your baby is ready to move on. Remember as well it's quite common to have to go back a stage if, for example, your baby has a cold or a growth spurt. Try to see this as a minor setback and keep the big picture.

What are the stages for gradual distancing?

Start by establishing a bedtime routine (see page 47), then put your baby to bed while he's sleepy, but not asleep. You will need to repeat the stages every time your baby wakes up in the night as well, which can be tiring.

Place your baby in his cot while he is awake and give him a nice cuddle while he's lying down. Then follow these stages:

Stage 1

Sit next to the cot and hold hands with your baby or lay him on your hand or arm. You can use your voice too to reassure him. You can pat him as well, gently so he knows you're there. Each night try to pat a little less. Stay in the room until he's fast asleep, then leave quietly. If you find he wakes as soon as you leave, try to wait 10 minutes, since that's about the length of time it takes for a baby to go into a deep sleep when nothing appears to wake him.

Stage 2
Sit next to the cot not holding hands or touching your baby, but stay in the room until he's fast asleep as above.

Stage 3
Move a little distance away from cot – maybe around a metre, but stay in the room. If he starts crying, reassure him, wait a little while, then move away again.

Stage 4
Gradually increase the distance by a metre or so each time, until you're sitting in the doorway.

Stage 5
As you progress, leave the room quietly as he's falling asleep, but stay near the door until he's asleep.

Stage 6
Leave the room completely while he is awake, but listen out for his cries on the baby monitor. If he starts crying, go back in, reassure him, wait a little while and leave quietly again.

Can I use gradual distancing to wean my baby off night feeding?
Yes, you can. Reducing the cuddles is easier than reducing the milk, so you can do that as a second stage. If you're trying to wean a baby off drinking milk before sleeping, it's OK to give him a little cuddle as he calms down – what you're trying to do is break the association with milk. Try to break the sucking association as a first step. Each step will take three to four days or more. Spend the first three to four nights letting your baby fall asleep in your arms – with no milk or sucking – then put him down in his cot. If he wakes up the second you put him on the mattress, pick him up again, and hold him for another ten minutes or so until he is in a deep sleep. This may feel like an eternity, but it's worth it

if you can lay him down without being disturbed. Repeat this every time your baby wakes up. Once this stage is established, put your baby in his cot when he is a little more aware of being laid down. As you start to break the sucking habit completely you can lay your baby down when he's awake, but stay in the room, following the stages above.

How can I do all this when I'm exhausted?
It's a good question. It's hard but it is also hard getting up four to five times a night to feed or soothe a baby. At least with sleep training you know you're heading in a direction that will hopefully mean you'll all be sleeping through the night sooner than you would be otherwise.

It's easier said than done but try not to plan anything you don't absolutely have to do while you and your baby are going through this time. If you have a partner or friends who can help by taking turns through the night, that's fine too – it doesn't always have to be the same person. So make sure you chat through what needs to be done in advance so it's clear what step you're at. Try to catch up on sleep at the weekends – it's almost like having a newborn baby again – but hopefully just for a few weeks until the new pattern has been formed. Good luck!

Is it bad to leave a baby crying?

Certainly a young baby, under the age of six months, shouldn't be left to cry at night. They still need lots of feeds and cuddling. Ideally they should be in the room with you. For older babies, the opinions are more divided and below are some of the issues that cause concern.

Parental bond Some experts believe that breaking the basic instinctive 'attachment' between baby and parent could harm the bond between them. They believe that this can then lead to impacts on the development of the baby as an adult. Certainly there are studies that show that poor attachment between parent and baby leads to higher incidences of harmful adult behaviour. In contrast, other experts say that 'behavioural techniques' cause no long-term benefits or harms to children, mothers or the parent-child relationship. However, these studies were quite short-term, so longer-term effects couldn't be considered.

Skipping feeds Sleeping for longer at night (in particular ignoring a baby crying until she goes back to sleep) reduces opportunities for breastfeeding. It should definitely never be done when a baby still needs regular feeds through the night. Skipping breastfeeds at night isn't only harmful for the baby – possibly leading to dehydration – but also impacts on your milk supply.

Does sleep training stress a baby?

A study was based around babies aged four to ten months, and consisted of researchers measuring the presence of the stress hormone cortisol in the babies' system. Cortisol at any elevated level, indicates that the baby is experiencing heightened levels of anxiety.

In the study babies' cortisol levels were measured as they cried themselves to sleep without being comforted. This study reported, on many occasions, babies who had stopped crying were still actually as stressed as they would be if had continued to cry. So they had 'given up' as opposed to settling. This is why we think it's okay to recommend gradual distancing, if absolutely necessary, but not controlled crying.

Chapter 4: Introducing solids

Introducing solid foods, also known as weaning, is a really important step in your baby's development and many parents are apprehensive about this big change. When you start off, try to look on it as a fun and experimental time. Don't rely on it for your baby's calories at first – it makes it too pressured. Keep the calories coming with breastmilk or formula, and have a relaxed time playing with new flavours and textures. The more fun your baby has with food, the more likely it is that she'll enjoy eating and allow you to present her with new foods that she will enjoy eating. Weaning will be a much more enjoyable experience if you can be relaxed and not worry about mess. Babies like to feel their food. They like to mush it in their hands, rub it in their hair and throw it on the ground. These are all very normal and healthy things to do. Your baby isn't being naughty – she's experimenting.

When should I introduce my baby to solids?

The World Health Organisation and the UK Department of Health recommend that babies are fed breastmilk exclusively for the first six months. You might choose to feed your baby formula instead. At six months babies should be introduced to solids. Some babies may be ready earlier, but they should not have solid foods before 17 weeks. These recommendations are based on research into the long-term health of babies weaned at different ages and with different foods. Before 17 weeks a baby's kidneys can struggle to process the waste products of some food and large food molecules may trigger an allergy (see pages 76-78). In the 1980s and 90s parents were advised to start solids at 12 weeks, but research has shown that this is not good practice.

It takes a full year for babies to develop all the enzymes needed for their digestive system: enzymes to digest starch develop at around six months; those for carbs by about seven months; and fat-digesting enzymes develop at around nine months. As a result even at the age of six months, there will be some foods that they cannot break down and digest. A young baby's digestive system is designed to process milk as his only food and breastmilk or formula milk provide all his nutritional needs. This changes at around six months, when the digestive system is ready for extra nutrients provided by solid food. For example, babies are born with a store of iron. After six months, the internal store will have run out, so a baby needs to start eating iron-rich solid foods.

When do I start my baby on solids if he was premature?
A premature baby may take a bit longer than six months to build the strength to be ready to try solids. It may be helpful to use your baby's due date as the guide, rather than his actual birth date. He is more likely to be ready nearer six months from his due date. However, don't follow this to the letter; watch for the signs that he is ready for solids – they will be the same as for a full-term baby, and you may delay it too long.

How will I know my baby is ready for solids?
Weaning is partly about a baby learning to move food around his mouth. Being ready for solids depends on both the maturity of your baby's gut and his physical development. Signs that mums and dads often mistake for a readiness are waking up in the night, wanting an extra milk feed, or chewing hands. Your baby is ready for solids if he:

- can sit up well in a high chair;
- can support and turn his head;
- is interested in your food – sit him in a high chair beside you when you are eating so he gets used to the idea;
- is ready and able to chew, and makes chewing movements;
- can move his tongue backwards and forwards to swallow;
- can close his mouth around a spoon;
- is beginning to develop the physical dexterity required to pick up food and put it in his mouth.

Your baby may not be ready yet if you offer a spoonful of food and he pushes it straight out, or if he closes his mouth and shows no interest in the spoon. The most important thing to remember is all babies develop at different rates and so you really have to look at your baby and assess whether or not he is ready. If the signs are there, go ahead, and if they're not, just wait a few days and try again.

Are there risks of weaning too early?
Yes, there are. Lots of people say that they introduced their baby to solids at say 16 weeks, especially your parents, and it didn't do them any harm. However, when you look at the statistics for big groups of babies who were weaned early, the risks can be seen. Babies weaned before they are physically ready for solids have a higher incidence of eczema, wheezing and chest infections. As we have said some babies are ready before six months, but it is important that you do not begin solids before 17 weeks.

Does it matter if I wait for longer than six months?
There are risks to not introducing solids to your baby until after six months as by this stage he is beginning to need the extra nutrients provided by solids foods. For example, if your baby is not getting enough iron-rich foods he can become anaemic, as his stores have run out (see page 61). Also, the development of your baby's oral motor control can be delayed if you wait too long to introduce solids. Advocates of the baby-led weaning argue that this method helps oral motor control skills to develop more quickly.

What is the best way to wean?
When it comes the time to wean your baby onto solid foods, bear in mind that there is a lot for her to learn, so don't expect it all to happen quickly. Your baby has been used to breastfeeding or drinking from a bottle since she was born. She now has to learn many new skills. She will experience new flavours and textures. She has to learn how to eat from a spoon, co-ordinate picking up food, chew and swallow food, sip from a cup, as well as eat with the family.

The most important thing is to be relaxed. With so many new to learn, things can get messy so try not to get upset when it does. Lots of parents feed their babies with nothing much on and put them in a bath afterwards!

Use the early days to experiment a little. Your baby may not eat very much at first but at this stage it's all about learning and the experience of new textures and flavours, not about calories.

How do I start?

Start with one meal, and follow it with milk afterwards to provide nutrition while your baby is learning to eat solid foods. Initially you need to see it more as developing skills and practising – rather than providing calories. Don't wait until your baby is hungry as he'll become stressed. Take it slowly and make it fun. Start with the new food – make it playful – then finish up with milk for the calories. Starting earlier in the day is a good idea as your baby is more likely to be awake and relaxed and you can watch for any reaction to a new food. Choose what suits you and your baby best. Later in the evening is not such a good idea.

What equipment do I need?
You will need a high chair with a tray that's easy to clean and have a ready supply of bibs. Plastic ones are good since you can just wipe them off afterwards, as are plastic bowls as they won't break if your baby grabs them and throws them on the floor.

How do I feed my baby with a spoon?
Make sure that the food isn't too hot; it should be just warm. If you want to taste the food to check the temperature use a separate spoon and never put it back in the food. Your mouth is full of bacteria that you could pass to your baby.

Use a small spoon and put tiny amounts of food on it to start with. Talk to your baby to attract his attention and make sure he can see the food coming towards him. Give him time to open his mouth, then gently put the spoon into his mouth and let him use his lips to take the food.

Is it OK if my baby wants to feed himself?

Yes, it's really important that in addition to spoon feeding you let your baby experiment with 'finger' foods to help him learn about tastes and textures. Put a range of soft and hard finger foods on your baby's tray. Be prepared for him to play with the food, try and feed himself or rub it in his hair; it's all completely normal.

Some mums don't spoon-feed their baby at all; see baby-led weaning below. A few babies won't put on enough weight if they only have finger foods. These babies can still keep on finger foods, but you need to supplement it with spoon-feeding purées. You can try letting your child be more independent again when he is stronger and hungrier!

How much should my baby eat?

Babies may not eat a lot at the beginning. Take it slowly and try to make it fun. It really depends on the baby and will vary enormously. Follow your baby's lead and gradually build to one meal, then two, then three. As his solid-food intake goes up, you can reduce the amount of milk you give him. Balance it out. By the age of about a year he should be getting most of his calories from solid food.

What is baby-led weaning?

This is a method of weaning that lets a child feed herself from the very start. Instead of spoon feeding purées and other textures, the child is given finger foods from the outset. This is fine if your baby copes with it and enthusiastically puts her food into her mouth, and you can see that she's growing well and putting on weight. Some babies don't put on enough weight with baby-led weaning – maybe they're not coordinated enough or just not enthusiastic about food yet.

How will I know when my baby is hungry?

The feeding cues will be the same as when he was younger. Your baby needs regular meals and snacks so don't wait for him to be really hungry before you offer him food. Try and recognise the feeding cues and have healthy snacks to hand. Always have a bottle of water and a soft-spouted cup with you as well. When your baby is hungry he may also cry and be upset, he might open his mouth very wide, smack his lips together or lick his lips, especially at the sight of food.

How do I know my baby has had enough?

Let your baby decide when she has had enough. She knows when she is full. Babies who are full often start to show less interest in the food, start eating more slowly, or stop opening their mouths as wide. Your baby may even close her mouth and turn her head away from the spoon. Some babies cry and become unsettled. Respect these signs of fullness and stop feeding.

What are the best foods to start with?

It's fine to let your baby do some baby-led weaning if you want to, but we advise to use purées of single foods for young babies to start with. Parsnip, sweet potato, courgette, carrots, apples and bananas made into purées with the consistency of smooth yoghurt are ideal. You can use the water you boil them in to make the purée thinner if you want to. Baby rice is also good. Once your baby gets more confident you can start combining foods to get a healthy mix of carbohydrates, protein and dairy. Lentils are a great source of protein and iron.

Are there any foods I shouldn't offer my baby?

If you are starting your baby on solids before the age of six months you should not offer cow's milk or dairy products, meat or poultry (including offal), citrus fruit, fish or shellfish, eggs, soya, nut products or any foods containing gluten, as your baby's digestive system is not mature enough to be able to process them.

Even if you start weaning at six months the UK Department of Health recommends that you avoid any unpasteurised dairy products, mould-ripened cheeses, foods such as homemade mayonnaise, cake mixture or mousses that contain raw eggs, undercooked eggs and pâtés to reduce the risk of food poisoning (see page 79). Any meat or fish should be well-cooked (see page 79). Don't add salt, sugar or honey to your baby's food.

Should I start by offering one taste at a time?

Yes, always introduce any new food to your baby on its own just in case his system cannot tolerate it. This is especially important if you have a family history of food intolerances or allergies. Some foods are so-called high-risk allergy foods, which means they are more likely to trigger a reaction. Examples of these foods are nuts, eggs, sesame seeds and dairy products.

What puréed foods should I start with?

Babies need to learn to use their jaws and teeth to break down foods and swallow the food safely. When you introduce solids to your baby at six months, she doesn't yet have control of her mouth and jaws, so she can't chew effectively. It's great for her to practice on finger foods, but her main nutrition should come from purées. The earlier you introduce solids to your baby, the thinner the purée it needs to be. You can prepare cooked or raw foods and purée them with a hand blender or mash them. Purées are a good way to introduce a huge variety of vegetables, fruits, carbohydrates, dairy food, fish and meat. Babies will eat and enjoy lots of different flavours, including fruit with meat and fish with cheese. Start with one food at a time, then start combinations. There are a number of suitable foods:

Baby rice This is a gluten-free first food especially made for babies, which makes an easy transition to solid foods as it can be mixed with her usual milk. Make sure you choose one that is sugar free.

Cooked purées Good choices for first cooked purées for your baby include root vegetables like parsnips, turnips, carrots and sweet potato. Apples and pears are good as they cook down quickly to become soft and easy to purée. You can boil, steam or roast vegetables or even steam them in a microwave.

Raw purées Good raw foods to purée or mash for your baby include the weaning superfoods such as avocados and bananas. Talk about fast food: simply remove the peel (and stone in the avocado) and mash with a fork. If you feel the banana or avocado is too thick, you can mix it with some expressed breastmilk or cooled, boiled water.

What are the best finger foods?

Giving your baby finger foods as well as spoon feeding can encourage him to feed himself. Soft finger foods are a really good option. Don't be too concerned if he doesn't chew it up and swallow it; it's more about getting the taste and texture. Putting the food in his mouth and spitting it back out is all part of the learning experience for your baby. He will make a mess, so be prepared for it. Start with soft finger foods and progress to harder fruit or vegetables that he can chew.

Soft finger foods These can be things like: hard-boiled egg, grated cheese, avocado slices, sliced fresh peach (take the skin off and remove the stone), mashed potato, boiled vegetables, cooled and sliced into fingers, such as carrots and broccoli.

Hard finger foods Once your baby is enjoying feeding himself with soft foods, you can progress to hard finger foods. These can be things like bits of apple, raw broccoli, carrot, cucumber or pepper sticks, steamed french beans, cooked spiral pasta, or fingers of toast with butter. You can also offer your baby some hummus that he can dip his hard finger food in. Remember always introduce new foods one at a time to check for allergies.

Why shouldn't babies have gluten before six months?

Introducing gluten too early increases the risk of a baby developing a gluten allergy, or coeliac disease later in life. Coeliac disease is an auto-immune disease in which the immune system attacks gluten in food that passes across the gut wall. It affects one in 100 people today. The current advice is therefore to not introduce gluten before the age of six months.

How do I introduce texture and combination foods?

One of the pleasures of eating is the combinations of textures, flavours and food groups that go together. Babies who are exposed to lots of variety at an early stage will be more open to eating a wide range of foods when they grow up, whereas babies who endlessly eat the same sweet baby purées will restrict their diet and their palate.

Fork mashing

When your baby's ready to move on from purées, he can move onto something a little bit thicker, with a little bit more texture. If you thought it was easy to purée baby foods before, you should see how easy it is to fork mash your baby's food. You can take a banana and a ripe avocado, chop them up in a bowl and simply mash them up with a fork. You can mix this with other purées or soft foods to alter the texture; for example, a little bit of yoghurt or some baby rice. Fork-mashing is great if you're away from home.

You can also mash anything that has been steamed or cooked. Fork-mashed food is a little bit thicker than purées and it does have some lumps in it, but that helps your baby develop. It's very important to move him on to different consistencies.

When should I introduce new consistencies to my baby?

It depends on when you started start weaning. However, when you introduce soft finger foods, try also feeding him foods with lumps. Your baby will enjoy lots of variety so fork-mash a little bit to spoon-feed your baby, and also offer the same food as a finger foods so he can feed himself at the same time.

Keep reintroducing foods. Don't assume that because your baby spat out beans once that he will never eat them again. A baby needs to try something a few times to get used to it. Give him time to learn about these new flavours and textures in a relaxed and calm environment.

When can I start combining foods?

Once your baby is used to single tastes, it's time to start combining foods so you can give her elements from all the different food groups in one meal. See pages 71-72 for more information on the food groups.

There's no right or wrong time. You can move to combination foods at any point. Most parents will start with a single food, just so that their baby knows what each taste is by itself. But as soon as you've introduced something as a single food, feel free to combine it with another food that your baby knows. When you're moving on to combination foods with your baby, you're going to find they are not going to be as thin and smooth as purées, but that's good. That's what you want. Your baby needs to get used to having thicker foods. You can always add more or less fluid depending on how thick you want to make it.

Making up a combination meal
After boiling green lentils for around 20 minutes, they will be lovely and soft. You can combine these with parsnip and couscous that has been forked and fluffed. This combination has a protein source, a vegetable source and a starchy carbohydrate. So in this one meal, your baby's getting a lot of what she needs. You can also add a little bit of milk to the mix, so she's also getting her dairy, which is fantastic. Using a hand blender you can bring together all the flavours and textures.

How can I prevent my baby from gagging and choking on lumps?

The gag reflex is very far forward in a baby's mouth. If a baby coughs and spits food up, it doesn't always mean he's choking. Gagging is his way of preventing himself from choking. That said, the gag reflex isn't perfect and babies can still choke. Be on the safe side and cut up food that is a hazard, such as grapes and blueberries, and never give chopped or whole nuts to a child under age of five years.

Many parents worry that their baby will choke on finger foods and they won't know what to do. It's important that all parents know how to save a choking baby (see page 118). We also recommend you do a recognised baby first-aid course so you are well-prepared.

Should I give my baby snacks in between meals?

Morning and mid-afternoon snacks are a great idea as long as they aren't salty or sugary. Healthy snacks can include things like pots of puréed apple, a banana you can mash, mashed avocado, finger foods like cooked pasta spirals, little sandwiches, a hard-boiled egg, boiled carrot sticks or pieces of raw vegetables dipped in hummus.

Should I give my baby water?

Always offer plenty of water as well. Give it to him in a soft-spouted cup and offer it during rather than before meals so that it does not fill his tummy and stop him from eating enough solid food.

What do I do if my baby becomes fussy or difficult at mealtimes?

All children have days when they don't want to eat, and other days when they never seem to stop. Many also like certain foods one day and they refuse to eat them next time they are offered. It is important to stay relaxed. Don't be concerned about what your baby eats in a single day – it's more important to view what she's eating over a week and balance it out. Keep a food diary as she may be eating more than you think. If your baby has a good balanced diet, is gaining weight regularly (check the weight charts in your red book), and is well-hydrated, then you don't need to worry. Try some of these strategies:

- If your baby has only one vegetable/protein/dairy/fat that she will eat, then stick with it, but keep trying to introduce new ones. It often takes many tries until a child decides she likes a new food. Never resort to adding salt or sugar because you think she may like it more.
- Don't force your baby to eat something she doesn't appear to like, and congratulate her if she tries it. Try offering it again another time.
- Try eating together as much as possible; you baby will copy you. Try asking someone she loves – for example, grandparents – to eat with you. Sometimes a child will eat for one person but not another. It's just a phase and it will pass.
- If she is difficult at mealtimes it may be because she is having too many snacks between meals.
- Keep portions small so your child doesn't feel overwhelmed and give

her lots of time to eat slowly. If she wants more you can give her a second helping. Don't rush her. Stay calm and do your best not to get cross.

What is a balanced diet for my baby?

Your baby's diet needs to include a range of foods from all the different food groups – carbohydrates, fruit and vegetables, protein, fats and dairy – in order to receive all the nutrients he needs. At this stage he needs to experience lots of different flavours and textures, and he will get a range of minerals and vitamins too. For the first months of a baby's life he will be getting all the nutrients he needs from breastmilk or formula. When a baby starts to eat solids it's really important to try and maintain that balance in the foodstuffs he eats.

Carbohydrates

These are one of the main nutrients. They are the most important source of energy for the body. The digestive system changes carbohydrates into glucose, which it uses for energy for your cells, tissues and organs. It stores any extra in the liver and muscles for when it is needed. Good sources of carbohydrates include: baby rice, bread, pasta, potatoes, couscous and rice. Wholegrain products are better than processed or white foods.

Fruit and vegetables

These are another form of carbohydrates and they are packed with essential vitamins and minerals when fresh. You can offer them raw, cooked, mashed, puréed or as finger foods. The important thing to remember is a good variety, with lots of different flavours, textures and colours.

Good fruits and vegetables to eat raw include: pears, mangoes, courgettes, orange pieces, sliced tomatoes, pepper slices, cauliflower, broccoli. Fruits and vegetables that make delicious purées when cooked include: courgette, carrots, pears, apples, broccoli, cauliflower, parsnips, butternut squash and roasted aubergine.

Finger foods include: carrot sticks; broccoli or cauliflower (boiled or steamed for around four minutes), green beans, corn on the cob (cook it, then cool it down by immersing it in cold water before you give it to your older baby to gnaw on).

Foods to mash include: bananas, ripe peaches or plums (skin and stone removed), figs, avocado.

Proteins
These play many critical roles in the body. They are the building blocks of body tissue and are needed for structure, function, and regulation of the tissues and organs. Great sources of protein include lentils, eggs, meat, poultry and fish.

Dairy products
These provide protein, vitamin D and minerals such as calcium as well as essential fats. Breastmilk or formula milk will provide your baby with most of his dairy needs, but other forms of dairy include cheese, butter and yoghurt, which you can use either on their own or as part of a recipe.

Fat
Babies need much more fat in their diet than adults because the fats are used for the development of their eyes as well as the brain and nervous system. Each brain cell is covered with a layer of fat cells that speeds up the communication between nerve cells. The body cannot make these fats and so essential fatty acids are a vitally important part of your baby's diet. Good fats can be found in lots nutritious foods such as avocados, oily fish, full-fat milk and cheese.

Should I give my baby low-fat or high-fibre foods?
No. Babies are growing fast, have small stomachs and so called 'diet' foods are not appropriate for them. They actively need fat for their development. See above. Also lots of low-fat foods are full of sugar, which is bad for babies. Instead, babies need small portions of fresh foods that contain lots of nutrients and calories. High-fibre foods are too rough for babies to digest so try to avoid these.

What vitamins and minerals does my baby need?

Babies are generally born with enough vitamin and iron stores to last them through the first six months of life. After this point stores run out and vitamins need to be supplemented through diet. If your baby is breastfed, you will need to start providing vitamin supplements, containing vitamins A, C and D when your baby reaches six months. These is available over the counter from your local pharmacy, but many health authorities offer children free vitamin drops, so ask your health visitor to see if your borough is one of them. The UK Department of Health recommends that all children be given vitamin supplements until they are five years old, regardless of their diet. If your baby is formula-fed, he will receive these vitamins from the milk. However, you will need to provide a vitamin supplement once your baby is on less than 500 ml (17.5 fl oz) of formula per day.

Does my baby need a vitamin D supplement?

Vitamin D is especially important in the first year of your child's life and is also one of the more difficult vitamins to obtain. While the summer sun is our best source of vitamin D, it is not recommended to leave babies or children in the sun for prolonged periods of time.

It is recommended that pregnant and breastfeeding women take a vitamin D supplement to ensure that their baby is born with enough to last until he is six months old. If you did not take a supplement during pregnancy and are exclusively breastfeeding, your child may be at risk of vitamin D deficiency and he may need a vitamin supplement from the age of one month. Talk to your dietician, health visitor or GP to find out if you, or your baby, are at risk.

My baby was premature. Does it make a difference?

Premature babies usually need to start vitamin and iron supplements earlier than six months because their reserves are lower at birth. Talk to your doctor or health visitor.

Will my baby need extra iron when he starts solids?

Iron is vital for the production of red blood cells, which transport oxygen around your baby's developing body. Babies are born with a store of iron that will last them around six months, along with the iron they absorb from breastmilk or formula milk. The iron in breastmilk is more easily absorbed, so formula has higher concentrations of iron to ensure enough is absorbed. After six months, a baby's internal iron store will have run out, so he needs to start eating iron-rich solid foods.

Iron deficiency, or anaemia, can be common in young children. For this reason it is really important to introduce your baby to iron-rich foods at around six months (and vitamin C-rich foods like citrus fruits to help iron absorption) when you start your baby on solid foods. Good sources of iron include: red meat, lentils, pulses and iron-fortified cereals (choose the unsweetened variety).

Will my baby need iron supplements?

Your baby may be prescribed vitamin drops with an iron supplement if you were iron-deficient during pregnancy or while you are breastfeeding, your baby was small for dates or he was premature. Iron supplements are necessary if your older baby isn't receiving lots of iron-rich foods. If you are exclusively breastfeeding and delay solid foods, your baby will be at risk of iron deficiency. Don't give your baby cow's milk until after his first birthday since it can interfere with his body's ability to absorb iron, and don't give your baby iron supplements as a precaution – too much iron is potentially harmful. If you're concerned, talk to your doctor or health visitor.

Can my baby's iron level be checked?

Yes. Your doctor should check your baby's iron levels with a blood test when he is 12 months old (or six months if he was premature). If the results show a shortage, an iron supplement and/or a boost on iron-rich foods may be recommended.

Is it safe for my baby to be vegetarian?

Yes, it is, but you still need to make sure your baby gets foods from all the food groups – protein, dairy, fat and carbohydrate. You also need to make sure she's getting iron rich-foods such as leafy green vegetables and lentils. Vitamin supplements are just as important for vegetarian babies (see pages 73-74). Keep a close eye on her development to make sure your baby is gaining weight in accordance to the weight charts in the little red book.

What's wrong with sugar?

High-sugar foods cause your baby's blood sugar to rise very quickly, requiring your baby's pancreas to release the hormone insulin quickly into the blood. Insulin initiates a process where the sugar in the blood is converted into glycogen and stored in the liver. This means that your baby will feel the symptoms of low blood sugar soon after eating sugar.

You probably recognise the unpleasant feelings of having low blood sugar yourself: feeling tired, irritable and lethargic. Similarly, your baby may well be cranky and go from high energy to sad or upset very quickly.

What are the best sources of natural sugars?

Your baby will get natural sugars in breastmilk or formula milk and in the fruit he eats. There's no need to introduce extra sugar from chocolate or squash into his diet. Instead, focus on foods that have a slow release of energy. Fruit is sweet, but it contains lots of fibre too, which means the calories and energy in fruit are released more slowly and steadily into your baby's bloodstream.

In contrast, fruit juices contain lots of sugar (fructose) but without the fibre in the fruit pulp that has been removed from the fruit juice. Giving your baby the actual fruit is a much better way to give him the vitamins he needs and introduce him to all their amazing flavours and textures.

Can I give juice in a bottle?

No. It's important to remember that nothing should be going into your baby's bottle besides formula milk, expressed breastmilk or water. You shouldn't be putting in drinks like fruit juice, fizzy drinks or squash into a baby's bottle as it's not good for his oral or general health.

Sugar in your baby's mouth can feed bacteria. The bacteria produce a plaque acid, which decays teeth; in severe cases decay results in the need for tooth extractions under general anaesthetic.

Many doctors and scientists are now reporting that the increased consumption of refined sugar in the Western diets (in foods like fizzy drinks, sweets, biscuits and ready meals) since World War II has in large part led to increased levels of obesity and type 2 diabetes (an inability to use the insulin the body produces).

What about fruit juice?
Ideally it's no fruit juice at all, and the best thing to do is stick to water. But if you really want to give your baby juice, then dilute it a lot. It should only ever be offered with meals and you must clean your baby's teeth afterwards. However, wait half an hour before doing this as sugar (even natural sugar from fruit) softens the enamel – so if you clean them straight away you risk destroying the enamel.

How can I avoid hidden sugars?
A lot of processed foods contain hidden sugars. The best way to avoid them in all our diets is to cook meals from scratch. There are many convenient, easy-to-cook meals based around fresh and frozen foods. Home-prepared meals can really help your baby to develop a love of healthy, freshly prepared food.

What's the difference between food allergy and food intolerance?

A food intolerance is much more common than a food allergy. The onset of symptoms is usually slower and may come many hours after eating the offending food. People can often tolerate a reasonable amount of the food, but if they eat too much (or eat it too often) they develop symptoms because their body cannot take it. An allergic reaction is more immediate, as the body makes actual antibodies to fight off the food. A severe reaction (anaphylaxis) can be life-threatening.

The symptoms of food intolerance may also last for several hours, even into the next day and sometimes longer. An intolerance to several foods or a group of foods is not uncommon, and it can be much more difficult to decide which foods or substances may be responsible.

If a person has an allergy to a food, he cannot tolerate even a small amount of it without suffering symptoms. It takes a tiny amount to trigger a response from the immune system. However, this makes it easier to diagnose.

If your family has a history of allergies, eczema or asthma, your baby will be at higher risk of allergies. If your baby has severe eczema before three months of age, she is more likely to be prone to allergies.

What are the symptoms of an allergic reaction?

If your baby is allergic to a food you may notice some or all of the following symptoms after she has eaten it. The reaction may not appear the first time a food is eaten. Symptoms of a mild reaction can include:

- flushed face and red, itchy rash, often with raised areas of skin (weals) and hives;
- red, itchy eyes;
- runny nose;
- abominal pain, vomiting and/or diarrhoea.

If there are severe symptoms you need to call an ambulance immediately and say that you suspect anaphylaxix. Call an ambulance if you notice any of the above symptoms combined with any of the following:

- difficulty breathing, ranging from asthma-like wheezing to gasping for air;
- obvious swelling of tongue and throat, which restricts the airways and leads to noisy breathing;
- pale, flushed skin;
- dizziness and confusion;
- collapse and possible loss of consciousness.

What are the symptoms of a delayed reaction?
Delayed symptoms can also occur and are harder to detect. These can include: eczema, reflux (see pages 107-109), poor growth, constipation and/or diarrhoea, frequent crying and seeming to have pain in the tummy area. Talk to your health visitor or doctor if you are concerned.

What can I do to minimise the risk of any reaction?
Introduce any new food to your baby carefully and on its own. For example, offer a tiny bit of cow's milk on a teaspoon the first time you give it and don't mix it with anything else. High-risk allergy foods include nuts, eggs, sesame seeds and dairy products. Always try the new food a few times before deciding it's safe. Remember a reaction may not appear the first time a food is eaten. If you think you baby has a food intolerance or allergy, talk to your doctor or health visitor about it.

What do I do if my baby has an allergy?
If you suspect a delayed reaction, start keeping a food diary and see your doctor. The food diary will help assess what's going on. If your child has a severe allergy you will be given an auto-injector containing adrenalin (epipen) to keep on hand just in case she comes into contact with the food stuff when you are away from home.

EGGS FOR BABIES

Hard-boiled eggs are a great soft finger food. Your baby can have fun picking it up and squeezing it. However, it is important that the yolk is hard-boiled if you are giving the egg to a baby under the age of one year; don't offer soft yolks until your baby is one year old.

Eggs are a high-risk allergy food so introduce them early in the day (rather than at her last meal of the day) and start by offering just a little bit, and check there's no reaction. Look out for a rash, lip swelling, vomiting, or your baby being unable to breathe (see page 77).

How can I make sure food is safe for my baby?

Young babies are still developing their immune systems, which will help defend them against germs. Until they're well developed, you need to protect your baby from germs so he won't get sick. Good food hygiene is very important. Wash your hands before preparing food, and before feeding your baby.

How can I prevent food poisoning?

Gastroenteritis is a nasty form of food poisoning that can make babies really unwell. Babies fed on formula milk are five times more likely to be admitted to hospital with gastroenteritis than breastfed babies. It's not necessarily because of the formula milk – although it can be because the milk is left too long before offering it to your baby (see page 35). It's usually because the equipment being used has not been sterilised properly. It's just as important to sterilise equipment if you are expressing breastmilk. To reduce the chances of food poisoning with solid foods for your baby:

- the Department of Health recommends avoiding unpasteurised dairy products;
- make sure eggs are hard-boiled as undercooked eggs with runny whites and yolks could contain salmonella bacteria;
- don't give your baby foods that contain raw eggs such as homemade mayonnaise, cake mixture or mousses;
- avoid liver pâté, raw fish and shellfish;
- ensure that meat and fish is cooked for the recommended time and at least until the meat juices run clear.

Can I share a spoon with my baby when feeding him?

It's not a good idea to share a spoon with your baby because you have a different selection of bacteria in your mouth. If you want to test the temperature of a food before offering it to your baby use a separate spoon and wash it up afterwards. If you want to encourage your baby to eat by copying you, pretend to take some food from his spoon.

How can I feed safely from baby-food jars?

Always check the lid of a jar – don't use it if the seal is broken. If you feed your baby straight from the baby-food jar, throw any leftovers away because the bacteria from the spoon can multiply in the jar. If your baby is unlikely to finish an entire jar, spoon some into a bowl with a clean spoon; then you can then replace the lid and keep what's left in the jar in the fridge.

Do I need to sterilise feeding equipment?

Before the age of six months all feeding equipment must be sterilised (see page 33-34). After six months, bowls, spoons and cooking utensils should all be washed in hot soapy water or a hot dishwasher cycle prior to use. It's a good idea to continue sterilising teats and bottles until your baby is a year old because of all their little nooks and crannies and the fact that germs grow quickly in milk.

Can I freeze baby food?

This is a great way to store freshly made foods. You can make up whatever you like – pasta sauces, soups, puréed casseroles and so on. You can make and freeze single fruit and vegetable purées that you then mix together later to make different flavour and texture combinations – such as adding apple and pear purée to fresh yoghurt. Or make chicken, parsnip and carrot purée to add to fresh pasta. Freezing homemade baby food has lots of advantages over buying jars of commercial baby food:

- Food will be a lot healthier and fresher.
- You know exactly what your baby is eating.
- There are no hidden salts or sugars.
- It's a great deal cheaper.

What's the best way to freeze baby food?

Make your purée, let it cool and then freeze it quickly. You can freeze in lots of different ways. To start with, try freezing small portions in ice-cube trays, then transfer them to freezer bags. Until you know whether or not your child likes a food, take only one cube at a time. If she loves it and gobbles it all up, you can always pop out another one.

When your baby is young, she might just have one (warmed up) cube of vegetable purée – as she grows she'll probably need a few. Alternatively you can freeze bigger meals like a puréed casserole into a plastic container with a sealed lid.

You can freeze pretty much anything. Milk products are absolutely fine to freeze, as are combination foods and family foods such as casseroles or soups. It is not recommended to freeze rice – cook it fresh and eat it immediately.

Label and date your trays, bags or boxes so you know what they are. Don't keep frozen foods for longer than three months

How can I defrost baby food safely?

You can either defrost your frozen cubes into a saucepan with a touch of boiled water to stop them from burning (stir it while it defrosts) or use a microwave. If you use a microwave, stir it thoroughly when you take it out, so there are no hot spots that might burn your baby's mouth.

Can I freeze combination foods?

Yes, you can make up batches of baby food from the different food groups and freeze them: for example, cheese sauce cubes, fruit cubes, chicken cubes. Then you can cook your carbohydrates (pasta or rice, for example) fresh for the meal and mix with your defrosted combinations.

Chapter 5: Day-to-day care

The learning curve with a newborn baby is very steep. Keeping your baby safe, clean and happy are all things you will get the hang of. Things like putting him to bed safely, bathing him, and changing nappies are all practical skills that will be second nature soon.

In this section, we cover the basics of nappy changing, clothing your baby, how to wash your baby safely and happily, how to soothe his teething woes and how to keep things safe around your home.

What do I need for my new baby?

You will need clothes, nappies, bedding and towels, a place for your baby to sleep, a pushchair or pram to take her out and about, and a car seat. Do plenty of research before you buy the bigger items.

You'll find you are given a lot of clothes when your baby is born, but you need the basics to start you off. Ask people for a range of sizes for the baby's presents – babies grow out of the newborn size every quickly and you'll want things to move on to. Try to assemble the following – either from hand-me-downs or new – before your baby is born:

- Six or seven cotton, all-in-one sleep suits (Babygros). Your baby will wear these everyday at first so a few extras mean you don't have to do a wash everyday. You can buy clothes in neutral colours if you don't know whether you are having a boy or a girl.
- Six or seven vests or body suits to go underneath the suits when it's cold. Buy the type that button under the crotch.
- Two wool or cotton cardigans or jackets.
- A wool or cotton baby shawl for when you take her outside.

- A broad-brimmed sun hat if it's summer.
- Warm outdoor clothes if it's autumn or winter – an all-in-one snowsuit or pram suit, a soft hat, mittens, socks or soft bootees.
- Several packs of newborn-size nappies, either disposable or reusable, or some of each (see below).
- Two to three soft cotton towels for after the bath.
- Muslin cloths – buy a couple of packs as you'll use them for everything, including protecting your shoulders from baby sick.

How should I wash my baby's clothes?

Young babies have very sensitive skin. Use a non-bio washing powder for washing your baby's clothes – biological washing powders are too strong. Avoid using fabric conditioner for the same reason.

Which nappies should I use?

There is no right or wrong answer to this question: as with most things, different styles suit different people. You can buy disposable or reusable nappies. We recommend talking to someone who has experience of using different types of nappies to help you choose the right system for you and your family, and you can also try to find a trial kit to test out the different styles available before your buy. You will get through at least ten nappies a day at first. If you are using disposable nappies make sure you have enough to enable you to stay in for the first few days. You'll need the newborn size to start with; some brands make smaller ones for premature babies.

There has been a revolution in the design of reusable nappies. You can use the traditional terry-towelling squares, which need to be folded in different ways depending on the size of your baby. Much easier to use, however, are shaped reusable nappies. Most involve a nappy cloth/pad that fits inside a shaped waterproof pant. They come in lots of shapes, colours and designs and generally have Velcro or press-stud fastenings to secure the nappy. Reusable nappies should be used with an extra disposable thin nappy liner that catches your baby's poo.

How do you wash reusable nappies?

You can wash them yourself or sign up to a delivery and collect laundry service. When you take the nappy off it needs to be soaked in a bucket of sanitising solution for a few hours (check the instructions on the solution). Most manufacturers recommend that reusable nappies are washed on 60°C (140°F) wash cycle using non-biological washing detergent; however, some of the nappy covers can be washed on a 40°C (104°F) cycle. Make sure that mobile babies, toddlers and pets cannot get into the nappy-soaking bucket; it's a potential hazard.

How and when do I change my baby's nappy?

Most new parents take a while to get the hang of changing their baby's nappy. Don't worry; it'll soon come naturally if you follow these guidelines. Lay your baby down somewhere safe, ideally on a changing mat on the floor. If you use a changing table, don't leave your baby even for a second, as she can roll off very easily.

From birth your baby will produce up to ten wet or soiled nappies a day. This slows down to around six to eight nappies a day when your baby is a bit older.

You'll get into a pattern quite quickly. You'll often see parents having a quick sniff of their baby's bottom (with the nappy on); it's a good way to see if something has been going on inside. If you're not sure, just have a quick look.

How do I change a disposable nappy?

Undo the tabs and gently remove the nappy. You can gently take the bulk of the poo along with the nappy, then wrap the nappy up tight securing it with the tabs so you can dispose of it without the poo going everywhere. Clean your baby's bottom with cotton wool and lukewarm water. Once your baby's bottom is nice and clean, lift up his legs and bottom gently, slide a clean nappy underneath and do up the tabs at the front. The nappy should be secured firmly, but not too tight.

How do I change a shaped reusable nappy?

Undo the nappy pants and the shaped pad. Remove the soiled liner (this can be flushed down the loo). Clean your baby as described previously and put on a clean nappy. Dirty nappies should be stored in the soaking bucket with a lid until they are washed.

How often will I need to change my baby's nappy?
With a newborn baby you should expect to be changing his nappy as follows:

- In the first 48 hours there should be around two to three wet nappies and several dirty ones. At first she will produce a dark-green or black, sticky poo called merconium.
- By day three or four you should be changing your baby up to ten times a day.
- By about day four or five your baby should be starting to produce yellow poo – at least two a day, plus some wet nappies.

Are there differences between changing boys and girls?

Yes, there are. With girls make sure that you use cotton wool and lukewarm water and you wipe from the front to the back to prevent any infection from her bottom going towards the vaginal area.

With little boys it's really important to make sure that you wipe all the little cracks and creases. Confidently and gently pick up the penis, move it out of the way, lift the testicles to make sure that you get underneath and get everything clean.

When putting on a boy's nappy, always make sure that the penis is pointing down towards the six o'clock position when you do it up. If it's pointing up to 12 o'clock he'll pee out of his nappy and all over himself and his clothes. If you point it to three o'clock or nine o'clock he can pee out of the side.

Watch out when you remove a boy's nappy, he might wee up and onto you – it happens a lot. Look out for it and be ready to catch it with a muslin or a nappy.

Should I use baby wipes?

It is best to clean a newborn's bottom with lukewarm water and cotton wool because of her delicate skin. If you do decide to use wipes it's a good idea to wait until after the first few weeks, and ideally only use them when you have to – for example, when you are away from home. When you do move on to wipes, make sure that you choose non-perfumed, alcohol-free wipes.

Do I need to use a nappy cream?

You don't really need to use nappy creams, particularly in the early days. Some people like to think about using a barrier cream to help prevent nappy rash. If you are using a barrier cream, make sure you use one that doesn't contain preservatives, additives or perfume. Just a thin, light layer is enough.

What is nappy rash?

Most babies get a nappy rash at some point when they are wearing nappies. It usually occurs because a baby is left in a dirty or wet nappy for too long. It seems to happen most in older babies who are on solids. Sometimes the cause is thrush or a bacterial skin infection. Some people think teething can cause nappy rash as well.

Symptoms The nappy area is usually red or pink in colour. There can be a patch of rash, or it can be spread over the whole nappy area. There might be intense spots, pimples and blisters. It's usually sore and warm to touch.

What to do Clean your baby's bottom with cotton wool and lukewarm water or fragrance-free wipes if you are out and about, then dry carefully. Leave your baby's nappy off as much as you can. Apply a thin layer of barrier cream before putting on a new nappy; don't use talcum powder as it can cause irritation. With home treatment, it should take four to five days to heal. If it is not healing or you are concerned, go to see your health visitor or doctor.

How can I prevent nappy rash?

This is much more effective than treating it once the baby has it. Keep your baby's bottom clean and dry by changing a wet or dirty nappy straightaway. Clean your baby's bottom thoroughly and let it dry before replacing a nappy. If the area looks a little sore, put a thin layer of barrier cream on the area before putting on a new nappy.

Why should my baby's poo look like?

Your baby's poo will change depending on what he's eating, whether he's well, and whether he's a newborn or a growing baby. Here's a guide to the different types:

Meconium Newborn babies produce a poo called meconium. It's made up of everything your baby was swallowing while inside your uterus, such as amniotic fluid and mucus. It's dark-green or black and sticky and it doesn't smell. If it doesn't appear in the first 24 hours after your baby's birth, see your midwife, health visitor or doctor. Your first milk – colostrum – works like a laxative for your baby and helps get all the meconium out of his system.

Breastfed babies Once the meconium is all out, your baby will have yellow, or slightly green poo. This has a creamy consistency, and looks a bit like mustard or korma sauce.

Formula-fed babies Formula milk isn't as digestible as breastmilk so babies fed on formula have thicker poo and are more likely to get constipated. The poo will be stronger smelling than breastmilk poo, and generally has a browner colour – a bit like peanut butter.

Weaned babies When your baby starts to eat solid food his poo will start to become more like an adult's. It is usually brown, thicker and smellier than poo from exclusively milk-fed babies.

Can the poo change?

Yes, if your baby is unwell or unsettled his poo may change. If in doubt, talk to your health visitor or doctor.

Green poo Occasionally babies produce a thin green poo, which can be quite explosive and your baby might be unsettled. If you are breastfeeding this might be a sign that your baby is taking too much foremilk. Try to encourage him to get to the thicker hindmilk by emptying the first breast completely before you offer the other breast. If you are bottle-feeding, green poo might also be a reaction to the formula milk. Green poo may also indicate that your baby has a tummy bug. If it lasts longer than 24 hours, take your baby to the doctor to be checked. You can take a nappy full of the green poo with you.

Diarrhoea Babies with diarrhoea will usually pass poo more often. It can be yellow, green or brown and might be very watery. Diarrhoea can spurt out quite quickly and it is more acidic and smelly than normal.

Constipation If your baby is constipated he will have hard, impacted or pebbly poo, which may be quite dry. If your baby has been constipated for longer than a day or two, go and see your doctor.

Poo with blood or mucus If you see any blood or mucus in your baby's poo or nappy take him to the doctor immediately (along with the nappy).

Very pale poo In a newborn baby this can be a sign of jaundice, so call your doctor or show the nappy to your midwife. In an older baby or toddler, pale poos that float can be a sign of illnesses like coeliac disease, in which the body produces an antibody to gluten in the gut. This may seriously damage the gut lining.

How do I keep my baby clean?

You don't need to wash your baby everyday. When you do, you can wipe the posset, wee and poo off with warm water and cotton wool ('topping and tailing'), or you can give her a bath.

Should I bath my baby as soon as she's born?

No, babies generally spend their first 24 hours learning to regulate their own temperature and so midwives avoid bathing them in that time. After that you might choose to bath your baby every day, but you certainly don't need to.

When should I bath my baby?
Every few days is fine. It is enough to top and tail daily. It really doesn't matter whether you bath your baby in the morning or evening. As she grows you can start including it in your bedtime routine (see page 46).

How do I top and tail my baby?
A 'top and tail' means giving your baby a quick clean at the top end and the tail end. The idea is to get rid of the daily possets, wees and poos, without needing to do a full bath. You need to use separate bowls of water for each end to avoid cross-infection. Cotton wool or a muslin works well – again use a separate one for each end.

- Start with gently wiping your baby's face with lukewarm water. Carefully clean all the creases around the neck where milk can quickly get smelly.
- Clean your babies eyes with cotton wool and lukewarm water. If she has a sticky eye, wipe the affected eye separately with cooled, boiled water and wipe from the inner side outwards (see page 115).
- Use the second bowl of water to clean your baby's bottom. Make sure you wipe your baby's back, and clean into the folds around her thighs.
- Wipe from front to back on a baby girl so you do not introduce poo into the vaginal area.

How do I bath my baby?
Here are some great tips on bathing your baby. Have everything ready before you start – clean nappy, towels, change of clothes, creams, changing mat before you begin – so you don't have to leave the room. Close the windows so there are no drafts. For safety's sake, ideally bath your baby on the floor in a baby bath, not up on a bench or table. However, if you have a bad back, for example, then use your common sense and bath your baby somewhere safe and secure for you both. Never to leave your baby on her own – even for a second to answer the door or your phone.

- Put the cold water into the bath first, then add the hot water until you get the right temperature. That way there will never be a bath full of very hot water, which is a huge safety risk. Test the temperature of the bath by either using your elbow or a specially designed baby thermometer available in most baby stores. Body temperature, or 37°C (98.6°F), is about the right temperature.

- The water should be shallow so there's no risk of your baby slipping under the surface.
- Gently lay your baby on the changing mat and undress her but leave her nappy on, then wrap her up in a warm, dry towel.
- Gently wipe her eyes, mouth, nose, ears and face with cotton balls or a muslin/soft cloth.
- Keeping your baby warmly wrapped in the towel, hold her so that her head is over the edge of the bath. Gently scoop water with the palm of your hand and pour it over her hair. You don't need any shampoo. Rub her head gently with the towel and place her on the changing mat again.
- Unwrap your baby, take her nappy off (clean her bottom if necessary) and pick her up again, ready to bathe. It doesn't really matter how you hold her, as long as it is firm and secure. Gently lower your baby into the water – keep a firm hold as she will kick about. Support her head and shoulders with one hand and with your free hand gently wash her, making sure that you remember all the cracks and creases.
- Take your baby out quickly so she doesn't get cold and quickly wrap her up again in a towel. Don't forget to dry in all the cracks and creases – especially under her arms and around her bottom, put on a new nappy and dress her quickly.

What should I bath my baby in?
Its best to bath your baby on the floor in a baby bath – but you can also bath her in the kitchen sink or a bucket, or a baby bath inside your big bath. Cover the hot tap with a cloth just in case. The main thing is never to leave your baby's side for one second.

Should I brush my baby's hair?

African American and Caribbean babies often have thick, curly or wavy hair that will need special care. Use a wide-tooth comb or soft-bristle brush and be very gentle with tangles. Comb out the hair when it's wet rather than dry, and use a little oil or cream moisturiser to help the comb go through smoothly. Caucasian and Asian babies have much less hair, generally speaking, and much less need of detangling.

Should I cut my baby's nails?

No, never cut your baby's nails (or bite them off). If they are long it's safest to file the nails down gently with a soft emery board.

When should my baby's cord fall off?

When most babies are born, a small clamp is put on a few centimetres from the belly button before the cord is cut. The cord can then be allowed to dry and fall off naturally, usually sometime between seven and 14 days, although it can also be a little earlier or later. Some parents worry that cutting the cord hurts their baby, but there are no nerve endings in the cord itself so don't worry.

Should my baby's cord be inside or outside the nappy?

Due to the position of the cord it can be tricky to decide whether to place the cord and clamp inside or outside the baby's nappy. It is up to you and what's most comfortable for your baby. However, if you do choose to keep the cord inside the nappy, make sure that the nappy waistband is not too tight as this may press the clamp against your baby's tummy, which may be uncomfortable.

How do I clean my baby's cord?

If the cord gets dirty from the nappy, this is not a problem and you can simply clean it with lukewarm water and cotton wool.

My baby's cord smells. Is this normal?

As the cord shrivels and prepares to detach, it is normal for it to be a little smelly. If the smell from the cord becomes very strong, and there is redness or swelling or some oozing from the umbilicus, this may indicate an infection and you should talk to your midwife or doctor. A short course of antibiotics may be necessary.

When does teething begin?

Teething occurs when your baby's milk teeth start pushing up through the gums. Some babies hardly seem to notice – whereas other babies will be really upset by the pain.

Most babies start to teethe at around the age of six months. However, all babies are different and there's a really wide range of time during which the first teeth will start to emerge. Some babies are even born with teeth. The usual range is between five to six months and a year – but it can be even later than that. But by the time your baby is two to three years old, she will probably have most of her teeth. Your baby's teeth will usually emerge in the following order:

- Two bottom front teeth (incisors) usually come through between five and six months.
- Two top front teeth (incisors) usually appear a month later around six to eight months.
- Two upper lateral incisors (either side of the first top teeth), come through between nine and 11 months.
- Two bottom lateral incisors (either side of the bottom front teeth), come through at ten to 12 months.
- First back teeth (molars), four in total, appear around 12 to 16 months;
- Canine teeth, the pointy ones, appear between the front incisors and the back molars at around 16 to 20 months.
- Second molars appear at around 20 to 30 months.

How do I know if my baby is teething?

With some babies, the teeth just pop through with no trouble at all. With other babies, however, there might be many different signs to show how uncomfortable they are. The symptoms may start to appear weeks or even months before the teeth finally emerge. The things you may notice may include:

- sore, swollen and/or red gums;
- dribbling;
- crying and fretting;

- rubbing ears;
- biting and chewing everything;
- flushed cheeks/face;
- not sleeping well;
- not feeding well – even refusing to eat at all.

Some people think fever, rashes or diarrhoea are symptoms too, but there is no medical proof that this is the case. If your child is suffering from any of these get advice from your doctor or health visitor.

How can I help soothe my teething baby?

You'll probably need to experiment a little to find out what works best for your baby. Here are some things that have worked for many babies.

Something cold to chew on Cool your finger under water and rub it gently over your baby's gums. You can buy a solid rubber teething ring. Sterilise it, then cool it in the fridge before giving it to your baby; don't use the liquid filled ones because they can leak. Or you can put a damp flannel in the fridge and let her chew on that (don't put flannels in the freezer as they may be so hard that they will damage her gums further). Make sure it's a clean new flannel that won't fall apart quickly when chewed, as the bits could be a choking hazard. A cooled dummy can also help.

Hard finger foods If your baby is over six months old and has started solids, you can give her lots of nice things to chew on. Avoid rusks since they're usually full of sugar. Try carrot sticks, cold bread crusts or apple. Always watch your baby when she has finger food in case of choking.

Cool water A sip of cool water can soothe the gums.

Baby teething gels If your baby is more than four months old, you can try rubbing a baby teething gel on her gums; some contain a mild anaesthetic to help with the pain (do not use adult oral gels). Other gels also contain an antiseptic to help prevent infection on broken skin. You can ask your doctor or pharmacist for advice. The effect usually lasts about 20 minutes, but you need to time it carefully since you can't use gels more than six times a day. Wash your hands thoroughly before you rub the gel on your baby's gums. Don't give the gel just before a feed, since the numbing effect means she might not be able to feed properly. Gels that contain 'choline salicylate' should be avoided since there's no evidence they work and there is a small risk of the salicylate leading to a serious liver condition called Reye's syndrome in children under 16 years old.

Teething granules Some parents swear by homeopathic chamomile powders, which you can buy from the chemist.

Distraction and cuddles It's an old trick but it often works. Try a change of scenery if your baby is very unhappy. Take her to the park in the buggy, or arrange to meet some friends. Try to think of something that's fun and different and will take your baby's mind off her sore mouth. Putting half of her toys away at any time is a great trick; that way so you always have a 'new' one to bring out. A cuddle can often work as well when everything else is failing. Try to sympathise – imagine a tooth breaking through your gum.

Pain relief If nothing else seems to work and your baby is more than three months old, give her the recommended dose of infant paracetamol or ibuprofen. Don't mix the two or increase the dose.

CRADLE CAP

This is a common and harmless skin condition seen on some babies' heads. It can be pale or yellowish in colour and scaly. It doesn't usually itch or cause any discomfort and it isn't contagious or a sign of infection. It usually clears up by the end of the baby's first year. In rarer cases it can last longer. Sometimes it occurs on a baby's face, ears, neck or in folds like knees and armpits.

What to do Don't pick it or it can become infected. Gently massage warm olive oil into the scalp to try to loosen it, then either wash immediately or leave overnight then wash her hair as normal. If it persist you can buy specially formulated shampoos in most chemists; make sure that your baby isn't allergic to any of the ingredients (some contain nut oils) and keep the shampoo away from your baby's eyes as it may have strong ingredients.

My baby has a rash on her chin, what can I do to help?

Try to wipe the teething dribble off your baby's face as often as you can with a clean muslin. Dab it off very gently; don't rub, as that can make the rash worse. You can also try putting on a barrier cream such as petroleum jelly or nappy cream to prevent soreness.

When should I start cleaning my baby's teeth?

As soon as your baby has teeth, you should start cleaning them. Use a muslin and water and rub very gently. As your baby gets older you can move on to a soft baby toothbrush and brush very gently.

How can I make my home as safe as possible?

As soon as a little baby enters your home, there are lots of things you need to be aware of as potential safety hazards. These hazards grow in number as your baby becomes mobile. Did you know, for example, that six toddlers are admitted to hospital every day in the UK because they've been so badly burned? Many accidents can be prevented by simply moving dangerous objects out of a baby's or child's reach.

Quite often, accidents happen because parents didn't know their baby or toddler could actually reach so high, or could open cupboards. Check every room in your home regularly and try to view things from your child's height. They grow up so fast, and you need to keep a step ahead at all times.

Kitchen Put cleaning products in a high cupboard, well out of reach; turn handles of cooking pots inwards, and ideally only use the rings on the back of the stove. Never have handles sticking out over the edge of the stove or work surface. Keep kettle flexes at the back of the work surface out of a baby's reach. Fit safety catches to all the low-level cupboards.

Bedroom Don't leave hair straighteners to cool on the floor and unplug electrical items. Keep your make-up out of reach.

Bathroom Put all medicines and bath cleaning equipment out of reach of children in a locked cupboard. Always empty the water out a bath and leave the toilet lid closed.

Sitting room Don't leave flexes trailing across the room; put breakables out of reach and make sure the furniture is sturdy enough and can't be pulled over by an adventurous baby.

Stairs Keep the steps clear of trip hazards. Put gates at top and bottom of staircases before your baby starts to crawl. Top gates shouldn't have a bar across the bottom – this can be a trip hazard for you.

What else can I do to safeguard my baby?

- Change your baby's nappy on a mat on the floor rather than a changing table – especially once she has started to roll over as she can fall extremely quickly.
- Keep plastic bags or nappy sacks in a high cupboard since they are a suffocation risk.
- Make sure curtain ties and blind cords are tied up well out of reach of babies and toddlers (or removed altogether). Make sure there are no cords near your baby's cot. It's all too easy for a baby to become caught up in these and there's a serious risk of strangulation.
- Always strap your baby properly into the high chair, pram or buggy. Never leave her alone in either of these.
- Hot drinks are a very common cause of severe burns. Never carry your baby with a hot drink in your hand. Put your hot tea or coffee out of your baby's reach.
- Don't leave your baby alone with a toddler, young child or pet.
- Don't ever give a baby a whole, spherical food such as a grape. Get into the habit of chopping them into small pieces. Children under five years old shouldn't be given nuts.
- Make sure your home is fitted with working carbon monoxide and smoke alarms. Put fire blankets and fire extinguishers in the kitchen.
- Go down on your hands and knees and pick up any small objects or toys that your baby could pick up and pop into her mouth.
- If you have older children, make sure their toys are well out of reach of the baby; these toys may have small parts that are a choking risk.
- When running a bath, always put cold water in before hot – that way there's no chance of putting your baby into water that's too hot.
- Stay with your baby every second she is in the bath – ignore your phone or take your baby with you to answer the doorbell.

How do I keep my baby protected from the sun?

A baby's temperature regulation system is not well developed and his skin is very delicate, so in hot weather he is at risk from sunburn as well as a prickly heat rash, heat exhaustion and more serious heatstroke. On hot days keep your baby in the shade, make sure your baby isn't wearing too many clothes (light cotton clothing is best) and that he has plenty of fluid or water to drink (lots of breastfeeds should be offered in this weather; see page 37, and cooled boiled water for a formula-fed baby; see page 38). If you are breastfeeding, make sure you keep yourself well-hydrated too. In hot and sunny weather:

- Don't ever leave your baby in a car, even with the windows open.
- Don't carry your baby for too long in a sling.
- Don't leave your baby's pram or car seat in the direct sun.

The sun is at its highest between 10am and 3pm, and at its hottest at around 2pm. You should be aware, too, that the sun can still burn through clouds and it bounces off snow, sand and sea.

How can I protect my baby from sunburn?

Keep a young baby out of direct sun at all times. Most skin cancers in adults develop as a result of sunburn experienced when they were young children. Be aware that a baby's skin is much more easily burned than adult skin, and babies with lighter skin, light eyes and hair are the most susceptible; however, babies with dark skin also burn. Remember you can't see sunburn happening. Below are some guidelines to follow:

- Babies under the age of six months shouldn't spend any time uncovered in hot, direct sunlight.
- If your older baby is running about outside you need to apply a baby-friendly sunscreen at least 15 minutes before he goes outside and reapply it frequently.
- Initial exposure for babies over about six months should start with a few minutes to a maximum of around 20 minutes in direct sunlight.

- Put a wide-brimmed sun hat on your baby that shields his face and neck.
- Dress your baby in an all-in-one UV-sun protection suit if he is playing in water outside; put on a legionnaire-style hat that covers the back of his neck with a peak to shield his face.

What is the best type of sunscreen?

Use a sunscreen or sunblock cream that's formulated for children. Chose one with a high sun protection factor (SPF), preferably 30, but many children's creams have an SPF of 50. The suncream needs to protect against both UVA (ultraviolet A, long-wave rays) and UVB (short-wave) rays. Look for this on the package.

If your baby has any allergies or is prone to eczema or asthma, he will be at increased risk of allergies to some creams. Test out a tiny patch of skin first and see if there's a reaction. Choose PABA-free, fragrance free, colouring-free suncreams for sensitive skins. PABA, or para-aminobenzoic acid, is an ingredient used in some cosmetics, which can trigger allergic reactions. If your child is playing in water, waterproof sunscreen is the best. Look carefully at how often you need to reapply.

What is prickly heat?

The symptoms of prickly heat (or millaria), include an itchy rash of small, red and raised spots that feel prickly, itchy or stinging. The rash can appear anywhere but it most commonly occurs on your child's face, upper torso and thighs.

In adults prickly heat usually occurs when we overheat and sweat. Babies can't sweat properly so their glands become blocked and the sweat gets trapped under the skin. If you suspect your baby has prickly heat, move him to a cool place, soothe the rash with calamine lotion and speak to your child's doctor. Watch him for signs of heatstroke.

What is the difference between heat exhaustion and heatstroke?

Heat exhaustion happens when the body loses too much salt through sweating. It generally develops gradually. Heatstroke is a potentially life-threatening condition that occurs when the body's temperature-control system fails and the body cannot cool itself down. The risk of both is much higher for babies than adults because their temperature-regulation systems aren't developed and they can't tell you they're too hot. Heat exhaustion can lead to heatstroke. Call your doctor if you notice any signs of heat exhaustion such as: loss of appetite, pale and clammy skin, possible cramps and weakening breathing and pulse.

Call an ambulance or take your baby to the hospital immediately if your baby has any of the following signs of heatstroke:

- a raised temperature (above 40°C/104°F); he will feel hot to the touch;
- diarrhoea;
- hot, dry skin;
- he is agitated or lethargic;
- he is having a seizure (see page 108);
- he is becoming unconscious.

SUN SAFETY AND VITAMIN D

Vitamin D is essential for good bone health and sunlight is the most important source. The time it takes for the body to make sufficient vitamin D varies according to a number of environmental, physical and personal factors, but is typically shorter than the amount of time needed for skin to redden and burn. Enjoying the sun safely, while taking care not to burn can help to provide the benefits of vitamin D without raising the risk of skin cancer.

Vitamin D supplements and specific foods can help to maintain sufficient levels of vitamin D (see pages 71-73) particularly in people at risk of deficiency. It is recommended that pregnant and breastfeeding women take a vitamin D supplement to ensure that their baby has enough stores to last until he is six months. If you did not take a supplement during pregnancy and are exclusively breastfeeding, your child may be at risk and may need a vitamin supplement from the age of one month. All children need vitamin supplements from six months to the age of five years.

Chapter 6: Baby health

Babies are born with a very immature immune system and they need to build up antibodies to protect them as they grow up. As a result babies are prone to coughs, colds, fevers, and all sorts of trials and tribulations. The good news is that this is all part of the process of building up their immune systems. One of the most important aspects of learning to be a parent is understanding what's normal, recognising when your child is unwell, and knowing what to do and who to call. As a mum or dad you are the best person to know when something's not quite right. Only you will know whether your baby's poo a bit runnier or harder than usual; whether she's a bit irritated or fractious because she is not feeling well. Would you know if she had a fever, do you know how to take her temperature? Would you know if that rash is eczema or meningitis? Widening your knowledge of baby and child health is a really important step that could save your baby's life.

How can I keep my baby healthy?

You can help your baby build his immunity to coughs, colds and tummy bugs and make him stronger by doing the following.

Breastfeed Guidelines suggest that six months exclusive breastfeeding is the best thing for a baby's developing immune system.

Take him outside Fresh air and exercise help babies sleep better and eat better, and therefore keep them stronger to fight off bugs when they catch them.

Let your baby get dirty After the age of around about six months you don't really need to be sterilising the cutlery and bottles that you're using for your baby but do continue to wash them thoroughly. You should continue to sterilise bottle teats until your child is one year old (see pages 33-34). Let your baby explore what's going on around him. Let him go out in the garden and get his hands dirty; the dirt, grass and air are vitally important for the development of his immunity and developing gut flora. There is increasingly strong evidence that children with reduced gut flora are more susceptible to eczema and allergies.

Give fresh fruit and vegetables When you start introducing your baby to solids, make sure to include plenty of fresh fruit and vegetables as they are full of immune-boosting vitamins and minerals.

Offer water to drink A baby's body needs to be kept hydrated and energised. Water is essential for delivering the nutrients that body cells need to stay healthy and ensures they are in a better state to fight off viruses and bugs.

Provide plenty of protein The immune system fights germs by multiplying its own cells, and to do this, it needs protein. So offer your baby protein-rich foods such as chicken, fish, eggs, lamb, lentils and other beans.

Cut out the sugar Many studies have shown that sugar – particularly processed sugar – suppresses the immune system. This is one of the many reasons babies don't need any additional sugar.

How can I protect my baby from serious illness?

You can immunise your baby against some of the illnesses that were once fatal, or left children with severe disabilities. Immunisations work by giving your baby's immune system a tiny weak or 'dead' dose of a disease – your baby cannot contract the disease from the jab as it is not active. Instead your baby's immune system recognises the disease and builds up antibodies to fight it. So if your baby or child comes in contact with another child who has, say measles, then your child will not get it. By giving her this protection, you are ensuring your child is safe.

Do babies really need to be immunised?

Some parents don't like the idea of immunising their baby. They don't like the idea of introducing a virus or bacteria into such a tiny baby, or don't want to see the child in pain. They may also think that if a baby is raised to be healthy and strong, with a good immune system, he won't get these diseases. The answer is that if you had total control of your child's environment, and he never came into contact with other children, animals, bacteria or viruses, then that theory might work. But the risks in the real world are too high, and the diseases he is immunised against are all potentially very serious.

For example, in the UK, the number of cases of measles cases rose sharply when a number of parents refused to allow their babies to be immunised against measles, mumps and rubella after a paper was published that linked the MMR vaccine with the incidence of autism. In 1996, measles had virtually been beaten, with a handful of cases around the whole country. By 2012, there were nearly 2,000 cases and the number was rising quickly. Measles is a highly contagious, unpleasant and potentially fatal disease. If a child does not have two doses of the MMR vaccine (at 13 months and before he starts school), he is at risk. The suggested link with autism has been completely discredited and it was only with a large public campaign to get children immunised, and for people to understand that the vaccination was safe, that the disease was controlled again.

When will my baby start his immunisation programme?

Your baby will be given his first vaccinations at the age of about eight weeks. This is often alongside his first developmental check. If your baby is unwell on the day, your health visitor or doctor may decide to delay the start until he is better. We have given the most up-to-date schedule, but this can change as more immunisations are approved.

At two months Your baby will be given three injections: five-in-one DTaP/IPV/Hib (this protects against diphtheria, tetanus, whooping cough [pertussis], polio and *Haemophilus influenzae* type b [Hib], a bacterial infection that can cause severe pneumonia or meningitis);

pneumococcal (PCV) vaccine; and a rotorvirus vaccine (a tummy bug that can make children very ill).

At three months He will have his second five-in-one DTaP/IPV/Hib and rotorvirus injections, plus meningitis C.

At four months He will have a third DTaP/IPV/Hib injection and a second pneumococcal vaccine.

Between 12 and 13 months He will have one injection immunising against MMR (measles, mumps and rubella), as well as a third pneumococcal (PCV) vaccine, a fourth dose of Hib and a second meningitis C injection.

At two, three and four years Your baby will be offered an annual flu vaccination.

At three years and four months Your baby will have a second MMR vaccine, plus a four-in-one (DTaP/IPV) jab containing diphtheria, tetanus, whooping cough (pertussis) and polio.

Is it normal for babies to get a fever after an immunisation?

Yes, it's completely normal. It's part of the body's fight against the disease. A low fever of around 38°C (100.4°F) is common for a short period following the immunisation and can be more likely after the second or third (booster) jabs. Some babies develop a fever within hours; in others it may be apparent a few days later. The injection site (arm or leg) may also be sore and your child may go off his food for a day or two. This is all completely normal.

You can give your baby the recommended dose of infant paracetamol to reduce the fever. Never exceed the stated dose. If you are concerned about your baby, ring your health visitor or doctor.

How can I tell whether my baby has a fever?

Normal body temperature is around 37°C (98.6). A child has a fever if her body temperature is higher than normal and is usually a sign that the body is fighting an infection. You will know how your baby's skin usually feels. If you touch your baby's forehead and she feels unusually hot, then use a thermometer to get a more accurate reading.

What should I do if my baby has fever?
Try to cool her down. Remove any warm bedclothes and dress her in light cotton clothes. You can give her paracetamol or ibuprofen (see page 105).

If there an obvious explanation for the raised temperature such as if you have a cold or an older sibling has one, then it's likely that your baby is suffering from the same viral infection, and it might not be anything to worry about. Babies can also have a mild fever in reaction to a routine immunisation.

You need to be much more alert and questioning if there's no obvious reason – especially if your baby is very young. If a baby under three months old has fever for no obvious reason, then it's important to call your doctor because it might be serious and you'll want to find the reason quickly. If your baby has a fever, together with symptoms like loss of appetite, cough, earache, vomiting, diarrhoea or she is not sleeping, then call the doctor straight away. Always take your baby to your doctor if her temperature is:

- 38°C (100.4°F) or over for a child under three months;
- 39°C (102.2°F) for a child between three to six months;
- over 40°C (104°F) for a child of any age;
- less than 36°C (96.8°F).

When should I worry if my baby has a raised temperature?
Your instincts will usually be right. If you're worried, call the doctor. Call an ambulance if your baby has a high temperature and there's a sign of a rash that you can't explain; it might be meningitis. Likewise if your baby has a fever and she is having any trouble breathing, call an ambulance or take her to your local accident and emergency department. If your baby is over three months old and is feeding and drinking well, call your doctor only if her temperature is more than 39°C (102.2°F) and lasts longer than 24 hours.

What happens if the temperature is lower than normal?
Your baby's core temperature can be too low and this can also be a problem. A temperature of less than 35°C (95°F) is hypothermia.

Your baby's temperature can fall rapidly if she has an infection such as meningitis and in some cases this can be a sign of septicaemia, or blood poisoning. Always call the doctor if your baby's temperature is lower than normal.

TAKING YOUR BABY'S TEMPERATURE

There are three basic types of thermometer. Digital thermometers are put under a child's armpit (don't put them in a baby's mouth), but take a few minutes to give a reading. A reading taken under the armpit will usually be 1°C (2°F) lower than normal. Strip thermometers can be put on a child's forehead. They are cheaper and easy to use, but less accurate. Digital ear thermometers are the most expensive, but give an accurate reading within seconds.

Can I give my baby medicine to reduce a fever?

If your baby has a very high temperature, you can give babies over the age of three months paracetamol or ibuprofen especially formulated for children. Younger than this, a baby can only have medication on the advice of a doctor. Follow the instructions on the packet and never exceed the stated dose. Even a tiny amount over the stated dose can be dangerous.

The medicine will bring the temperature down – so there's a risk you might mask an underlying problem, which is why it's so important to find out why your baby has the high fever. If there's no obvious reason for the fever, take your baby to the doctor straight away. If you keep medicating, and your baby's temperature seems to drop, you may not be aware of something more serious.

What causes diarrhoea and vomiting?

Vomiting and diarrhoea in babies are often caused by gastroenteritis, which is usually the result of a virus. It is potentially serious in children as they can lose a lot of fluid from the body very quickly and become dehydrated – which, if left untreated, can be fatal. The loss of fluid means important salts (electrolytes) are lost from the baby's body.

Most cases of gastroenteritis in children are caused by rotavirus. If a baby has had rotavirus once, his system starts to build up antibodies against it and he will become immune to it. In the UK an oral vaccine for rotavirus is now offered as part of the baby's immunisation programme (see page 103). Salmonella poisoning is another common cause of gastroenteritis. Breastfed babies get these tummy bugs less often than bottle-fed babies.

How can I help my baby?

It's vital to keep your baby hydrated; offer him frequent feeds as normal. Diarrhoea is easier to look after because you can continue to give the baby fluid through his mouth. If you are concerned, call your doctor or health visitor for advice.

Always call the doctor if your baby vomits three or more times in 24 hours, or has six or more nappies with diarrhoea. If your doctor recommends it, you can give oral rehydration fluids or salts that help replace some of the electrolytes lost during vomiting and diarrhoea. You can buy them from a pharmacy or your doctor may give you a prescription.

If your baby is vomiting and has a fever, seek medical advice quickly. If your baby has a sunken eyes and/or fontanelle (the soft spot on the top of the head), he is severely dehydrated and needs urgent medical attention so call an ambulance. He may have an underlying infection or, in a severe case, meningitis (see page 112). Your baby may be becoming dehydrated if he is unwell and:

- is producing fewer wet nappies a day than normal;
- is vomiting and or is producing nappies with diarrhoea;
- has lost his appetite;
- is just not himself;
- is not producing tears when crying;
- has a dry mouth or tongue;
- has loose, pale or mottled skin;
- has cold hands and feet;

Your baby is suffering from severe dehydration and requires urgent medical help if he has vomiting and/or diarrhoea and:

- seems listless and floppy;
- seems lethargic or irritable;
- has a sunken fontanelle (the soft area on the top of his head);
- has sunken eyes.

How can I prevent the bug from spreading?

Make sure everyone washes their hands using warm, soapy water before touching him. Keep the nappy changing area clean and wash his clothes, towels and bedding frequently on a hot 60°C (140°F) cycle. Keep your baby away from nursery and playgroups for 48 hours after recovery and don't take your baby into a swimming pool for two weeks after the last bout of diarrhoea.

How can I minimise the chance of my baby catching a tummy bug?

Keep your baby well away from anyone suffering from a gastric bug as they are easily spread from one person to another, especially young babies and children. If you bottle-feed your baby, make sure that all equipment is properly sterilised (see pages 33-34). Once your baby is weaned, wash your hands before feeding and keep all equipment clean (see pages 79-80).

What is reflux?

Reflux occurs when the contents of the baby's stomach, such as milk or acid, come up the feeding tube towards the baby's mouth. Most babies have a little bit of reflux, because the valve at the end of the food pipe, which is like a door into the stomach and designed to keep the food down, hasn't fully developed. So lots of babies do something called 'posseting', which means a little bit of milk comes back up when they burp. This is normal and very common.

It's only when strong acid comes back up from the baby's stomach that it isn't normal and it can be very painful. The good news is that 'the valve door' gets stronger through the first year, so the chances of the

FEBRILE SEIZURES

Some babies develop seizures when they have a very high temperature. This happens because the body's system can't deal with the high temperature. Your baby is having a seizure if he is very hot, looks flushed, and starts shaking vigorously and arching his back. Cool him down as quickly as possible: remove his bedding and undress him down to his nappy (you may need to wait until he stops shaking). Put pillows around him to protect him but don't restrain him in any way. Open the window to make sure cooler air is circulating. **Don't** sponge him with tepid water as you may cool him too quickly. When the seizure stops he may fall asleep, so lay him on his side. Call your doctor as soon as possible (or an ambulance if this is the first fit he's ever had). A child who has had one seizure is likely to have another next time he has a raised temperature.

reflux going away naturally increase as the baby grows. It's more of a problem in young babies who are still exclusively milk fed and who tend to spend more time lying down; it's less of a problem once babies sit up more and go on to solid feeds.

Your baby may have reflux if: she shows signs of pain or discomfort when feeding, such as arching her back, refusing milk and crying; frequently vomits or spits up a lot of her milk; coughs frequently, including at night, but with no sign of a cold; wakes often at night, especially about 45 minutes after she fell asleep; she is not gaining weight (and may even be losing it). Always talk to your doctor and health visitor if you suspect reflux.

What can I do to help reflux?

Feed little and often, so your baby's tummy doesn't get too full. It can help to prop your baby up after a feed at a 45-degree angle in a baby chair, or just sit her on your lap for at least half an hour after each feed to allow the milk to settle into her stomach – longer for formula milk since it takes longer to digest. It can also help to prop the head end of your baby's cot up a bit so that her head is slightly raised compared to the rest of her body.

Don't dress your baby in clothing that is tight around her tummy as it can push the stomach contents back up. It can help to carry your baby in a sling, which will keep her upright, and minimise time in her car seat or buggy where she can slump into an uncomfortable position.

How can I look after my baby if he gets a cough or cold?

Babies and young children haven't yet built up immunity to all the different types of coughs and colds that go around, so they can get them quite a lot. As they build their immunity, they'll be able to fight them off better and better.

Sometimes even a healthy immune system – particularly a baby's – will still be overcome by a cold and you'll need to soothe him while he is unwell. It can be difficult when a baby's nose is very blocked. There are sucking devices that can help. Some mums swear by sucking the mucus out with their own mouths. It's up to you which method you use, the only guideline is to be very gentle and do the following:

- Increase the amount of water he is drinking.
- If the child has a fever or discomfort, the recommended dose of infant paracetamol or ibuprofen can help (never give them together unless advised by a health professional). Always follow the instructions very carefully.
- Make sure everyone in the family washes their hands frequently so germs don't spread.

Should I ask for antibiotics when he has a cold?

No. Asking your doctor for antibiotics every time your baby has a cold or a sore throat is not a good idea; most doctors won't prescribe them anyway. Colds and coughs are mostly caused by viral infections. Antibiotics treat only illnesses caused by bacteria. Bacteria will grow bigger and stronger if consistently exposed to antibiotics, so it becomes harder and harder to treat, say, a bacterial ear infection that develops later. Antibiotics can also wipe out the natural flora in your baby's gut, which can really harm his digestive system and possibly even lead to the onset of allergies, asthma and eczema.

What do I do if my baby has a sore throat?

Sore throats are a common partner of a cold. They are usually viral and start a day or two before the cold emerges. The recommended dose of infant paracetamol or ibuprofen can be used in moderation to ease the discomfort.

Most sore throats will clear up on their own – like the cold does. But if they last longer than about four days, or your child also has a temperature, or is unable to swallow fluids, go and see your doctor.

What do I do if my baby is coughing all the time?

We cough when mucus trickles down our throats and we try to clear it away. Babies are much less efficient at getting the oxygen they need and long bouts of coughing will exhaust them. If a baby's cough seems bad, or has lasted a long time, then do go and see your doctor.

If your baby is coughing so much he's having trouble breathing, his nostrils are flaring, and/or you can see his rib shape as he breathes and coughs, then go to the hospital or call an ambulance.

If your baby is coughing a lot, especially at night, you can try raising the head end of the cot by putting books under the legs until it reaches an angle of about 45 degrees. This is also advised for babies with reflux.

Could the cough be something more serious such as asthma or croup?

With both of these conditions your child may be coughing, but may also have difficulty breathing, so if in doubt call your doctor, or take your child to the local accident and emergency department.

What is asthma?

This is condition in which the muscles in the air passages in the lungs narrow and make breathing difficult. It is often triggered by an allergic reaction to something such as dust or pet hair, for example.

There is no one test to diagnose it, but if a baby is coughing for no apparent reason, especially at night or in the morning, or appears to be wheezing, she may have it. It is more common if there is a family history of it. If you are unsure, see your doctor. If asthma is confirmed, your baby may be given a special inhaler.

What is croup?
This is caused by an inflammation of the windpipe (the main breathing tube to the lungs). Symptoms include a distinctive 'barking' cough, croaky voice, and your baby may appear to make a raspy sound known as stridor when she breathes in. It most often occurs at night and the child may struggle to breathe. Croup can be scary for you, but it can be treated at home. Sit your child upright on your lap and keep her as calm as possible, as breathing is more difficult if she's distressed. Give fluids to prevent dehydration and keep her cool. Call your doctor if you are worried, and always if your child also has a high fever.

How can I prevent constipation?

About one in three babies or toddlers will have constipation at some point. If your baby is not pooing every day, and when he does it he is straining to get it out, his poo is hard and dry, or the poo is in balls, he is constipated. Breastfed babies rarely get constipated. It's more likely in a bottle-fed baby or babies who have started on solid food. If your baby is on solids or formula-fed aim to do the following things:

- Make sure he has plenty of liquids and try increasing fluids by offering extra water between meals.
- Increase his intake of fruit. Try apple, plums, prunes, apricots, peaches or raspberries. Baked beans, frozen peas and sweetcorn are good sources of fibre. A little fresh orange juice in your baby's water can help soften stools.
- Get him moving as much as you can.
- Gently massage his abdomen in a clockwise direction or gently move his legs – bending his knees and gently rotating in a clockwise direction may also help stimulate bowels.

My baby doesn't want to poo as his bottom hurts. What can I do?
For some babies their bottom really hurts when they are constipated and they worry that it might happen again, so they try not to poo. If this happens, do everything you can to make sure your baby's fluid intake is sufficient, and his diet is good so the stools become soft. Talk to your doctor or health visitor as this problem can get worse quite quickly. It is important that your child poos regularly – but this might not be every day; it's the consistency that matters.

Resist the temptation to give your child laxatives. Try everything you can to sort out the problem with diet and water. If you start your child on laxatives, he may become dependent on them to poo. This dependence can last for years. In really severe cases, you might need to use laxatives for a short time, but get the diet and fluids balanced and wean him off them as quickly as you can. Never leave constipation untreated. Go to your doctor or health visitor as soon as possible. Chronic constipation is a real issue and can be very serious – and even lead to conditions like septicaemia (see page 115).

Are there more serious reasons my baby might be constipated?
Very rarely constipation is caused by other underlying conditions including spinal cord abnormalities, malformed anus and rectum, Hirschsprung's disease, which affects the bowel, making it difficult to pass stools, and cystic fibrosis. Any of these conditions, if suspected, must receive immediate medical attention.

What is meningitis?

This is a very serious infection of the layers (meninges) that surround the brain and spinal cord. It can be caused by a viral or a bacterial infection and it can lead to potentially fatal septicaemia (blood poisoning), also known as sepsis. Familiarise yourself with potential symptoms and signs. If you suspect your baby has meningitis or sepsis, don't wait for all the symptoms to appear – call an ambulance or take your baby to your local hospital accident and emergency department quickly.

How to recognise meningitis

Symptoms can appear in any order, the rash might not appear, and the early symptoms are easily mistaken for a cold or flu. They include:

- flu-like illness with a high fever;
- cold hands and feet;
- pain/irritability from muscle aches or severe limb/joint pain;
- blotchy, mottled or pale skin;
- vomiting and sometimes diarrhoea;
- sensitive eyes to any light (daylight, TV or electric light);
- staring;
- floppiness;
- staring;
- stiffness with jerky movements;
- fast, shallow breathing or difficulty breathing;
- blue tinge around the lips;
- extreme shivering;
- sleepy, difficult to wake up, or unresponsive;
- a stiff neck;
- a tense or bulging soft spot on the head (fontanelle);
- a high-pitched or moaning cry in a young baby;
- 'pin prick' rash/marks or purple 'bruises' on the skin, which don't go away if pressed. These could be the last symptom to develop and it's the most serious as it's a sign of septicaemia (see below). If you see this, call an ambulance.

What are the signs of septicaemia?

In the early stages, it is often hard to distinguish common viral infections from septicaemia. If any of the symptoms above exist and your baby has cold, pale skin with strange colours or markings so she appears 'mottled' and is unresponsive then you should take her to hospital or call an ambulance without delay. If a baby has two or more of the following symptoms she may have sepsis:

- a very high or very low temperature (low temperature in the extremities can mean that the body's circulation is 'shutting down');

IDENTIFYING A MENINGITIS/SEPTICAEMIA RASH

This rash is usually flat and a deep red/purple colour, and is non-blanching (it does not disappear when it is pressed). It generally starts as tiny spots but these can quickly grow. If your baby does get a rash and you're not sure whether it's meningitis, quickly do what's called the 'glass test'. There are other types of rashes that are non-blanching, but don't take any chances by guessing.

Pick up a smooth-sided glass (one without a pattern). Push the side of the glass down against the baby's rash, and roll the glass along the rash.

- If the rash disappears it is an ordinary rash – perhaps eczema.
- If the rash does not disappear it is a 'non-blanching' rash and you need to get your baby to your local hospital quickly. Call an ambulance or take him yourself if there is a delay.

- a sunken fontanelle ('soft spot');
- rapid shallow breathing;
- listlessness and lethargy;
- crying inconsolably;
- dry nappies.

What is eczema?

Atopic eczema usually occurs when there's a family history of allergies such as eczema, asthma or hayfever, and it affects over 12 percent of children. Baby eczema can be difficult to treat. It usually starts in the early months, but the good news is that children often grow out of it.

What are the symptoms?

In fair-skinned children, eczema presents as patches of red, dry and itchy skin on the face or behind the ears or in the creases of the neck, knees and elbows. In Asian and darker-skinned children, eczema may not affect body creases, but may appear on other parts of the body.

How can I help my baby?
Keep your baby's nails short to prevent him from scratching the itchy skin and causing infection. Puts mitts on him if he scratches a lot, especially when he's asleep. Bath him everyday in luke-warm water and don't add soap or bubbles. Moisturise him skin afterwards – use plain, perfume-free moisturiser. Your doctor may recommend a suitable type.

Dress your baby in organic, pesticide-free cotton clothing – avoid wool or artificial fibres. The same goes for his sheets and bedding. Wash clothes and bedding in non-biological detergent and don't use fabric conditioner. Keep the bedroom cool and clean it regularly to minimise dust mites and shut pets out of his room.

If the eczema is still not improving, your doctor may prescribe steroid cream as a last resort. Cut out processed sugars completely as these can make eczema flare up. It can help to reduce dairy products or even cut them out of your child's diet, but don't do this without talking to your doctor or a dietician as they contain essential proteins and vitamins.

Some eczemas improve if exposed to chlorine in a swimming pool, whereas other types are made worse. If the eczema is helped, swim regularly. If it is irritated, either don't swim, or if you do, rinse your baby's skin very thoroughly and moisturise immediately after.

My baby has sticky eye, what should I do?

Sticky eye is very common in young babies. The tear ducts from the corners of the eyes to the nose are usually narrower in newborn babies. They can be slightly blocked, causing accumulation of tears in the corners of the eye, making it watery. When the tears dry up, the eyes will look 'sticky'. The yellowish, sticky substance can sometimes be quite crusty or flaky, especially after sleeping.

What can I do to help?
Clean your baby's eyes very gently with cotton wool soaked in cooled, boiled water. Wipe from the inner side of the eye outwards and use a new piece of cotton wool for each stroke. Don't let any water trickle cross the bridge of the nose into the other eye, as it could infect the other eye.

If the skin around the eye, the eyelid or the eyes themselves look red or sore, if the discharge is yellow or green and becomes more severe take your baby to your doctor as it may be conjunctivitis, an infection that may need antibiotics.

What do I do if my child injures himself?

Knowing what to do if your child is injured can save his life. It's important to stay as calm as you can so as not to panic your baby. It is well worth going on a first-aid course before your baby is born (or soon afterwards), so that an expert can show you some essential life-saving skills then you'll know what to do in an emergency. Several organisations run courses specially aimed at parents. Here are some general guidelines but always call an ambulance for your child if he:

• is unconscious;
• is having difficulty breathing (either breathing fast or panting, or he is wheezy), or has stopped breathing or is struggling for breath (you may notice his skin being sucked in under the ribcage);
• has a seizure for the first time, even if he seems to have recovered;
• has a cut that won't stop bleeding;
• has a leg or arm injury and can't use the limb (don't move your child unnecessarily and support the limb with your hands or a rolled-up towel while you wait for help).

What should I do if my child cuts himself?

Children often fall and cut themselves and most of these injuries can be safely treated at home. Your main aim is to control the bleeding, especially if the bleeding is severe.

What to do For minor injuries, clean around the wound and protect the injury with a plaster to keep it clean. If there is dirt in the wound rinse it under cold running water. If there is any gravel stuck in the cut, take your child to the nearest walk-in clinic; don't try to remove it yourself.

If it is a large wound, and/or there is serious blood loss, place a sterile dressing pad over the wound and press directly over the injured area. If you don't have a dressing with you, apply direct pressure over a clean muslin, nappy or article of clothing. If you have nothing, then use your bare hands. Hold the wound above the level of the child's heart to slow down the blood flow to the area. Secure the pad with a bandage and call an ambulance or get someone to take you both to your local hospital while you continue treating your child.

My child has a burn. What do I do?

This is one of the most common accidents for babies and toddlers. There are three levels of severity of burn. A superficial burn, which is just a bit red and a bit sore; a partial-thickness burn, which will be reddened and blistered; and a full-thickness burn, which may be blackened or charred or may be white and/or waxy. The two serious risks with burns are infection and fluid loss, especially if the burn covers a large area.

What to do Hold the burn under cold water for at least ten minutes to stop the burning process (this is a lot longer than you'd imagine – so time it). If you stop too soon, the skin tissue deep down will still be burning. Cover with plastic kitchen film, not a fluffy bandage; but don't wrap it right around the limb as burn injuries may swell. Never break a blister caused by a burn – you may introduce infection – and never use butter or toothpaste on a burn.

All burn injuries on babies and young children need to be assessed by a doctor. Go straight to your local hospital if the burn is full-thickness, even if it is very small, and/or larger than one percent of the size of the body (equivalent to the palm size of the hand).

What do I do if my baby is stung by a bee or a wasp?

These can be very painful, and in the case of bee sting the barb may be visible in the skin. If you have a family history of allergies, your baby is at greater risk of being allergic to bee stings. Talk to your doctor about this. If you baby has a known allergy and you have been prescribed an epipen for use in the event of a serious allergic reaction, you should carry it with you at all times.

What to do Scrape the sting off the skin with a piece of stiff, thin card. Wrap a bag of ice in a cloth and hold it against the area to prevent swelling. If your baby is at risk of allergy you may need to give him the recommended dose of antihistamine syrup. Keep the epipen handy.

What do I do if my baby is choking?

Babies are always putting things in their mouths and can easily choke on small pieces of food or little bits of their older siblings' toys.

What to do If your baby is coughing and able to cry or make a noise, leave him alone. If he is unable to make a noise, lay him face down across your lap. Support his head and shoulders with one hand and with the heel of your other hand give him five sharp back blows between his shoulder blades. Turn him over on your lap and check his mouth; remove anything obvious. If the blockage is still there, try chest thrusts. Place two fingers on the lower part of his breastbone just below the line between his nipples. Press inwards and downwards, towards his head up to five times. Check his mouth again. If the blockage is still there, repeat the back blows, mouth check and chest thrust three times, then call an ambulance if this has not already been done. Keep going with the treatment until the ambulance arrives. If your baby loses consciousness, treat as described below.

I think my baby is unconscious. What should I do?

To find out whether your baby is really unconscious, you need to see if you can get a response. You can try talking to him or tapping his shoulder. If that doesn't work, trying flicking the sole of his foot as that is more sensitive. If there's no response, then your baby is unconscious.

Check breathing First check whether your baby is breathing. Lay him on his back on a firm surface. When he's unconscious he has no muscle control so his tongue can fall back and block the air passages to the lungs. Place one hand on the baby's forehead and one finger of your other hand on the point of his chin. Tilt the head back slightly – but not too far – and lift the chin. A baby's airway is a little bit like a drinking straw. If you tilt the head right back you'd close the airway again. Tilting the head lifts the tongue away from the back of the throat so he may be able to breathe. Bend down and put your ear next the baby's mouth and nose and listen and feel for normal breaths against your ear and look for chest movement – but for no longer than ten seconds.

If the baby is breathing Ask someone else to call an ambulance. If you are on your own, hold your baby in the recovery position first.

Cradle your baby so that his head is lower than his body, support his head and keep it tilted slightly back so that any saliva or vomit can drain from his mouth. Wait for the ambulance to arrive, but keep checking to see he is breathing.

If the baby is not breathing You need to start a combination of rescue breaths and chest compressions (cardiopulmonary resuscitation/CPR). Make sure your baby's head is still tilted back slightly, look in his mouth and remove anything obvious. Take a normal breath, put your mouth over the baby's mouth and nose, then breathe out, watching to see his chest rise. Remove your mouth and watch her chest fall. Repeat this to give five rescue breaths. Put two fingers on the centre of the baby's chest on the breastbone – between his nipples. Keeping your fingers straight, press down vertically on the chest, depressing it by one-third of its depth, then release the pressure but don't remove your fingers. Repeat to give 30 compressions at a rate of about 100-120 per minute (roughly to the beat of the Bee Gee's song 'Stayin' Alive'). After 30 compressions, give two more rescue breaths. If you are on your own, do this for one minute before calling the ambulance. Continue CPR until the ambulance arrives or your baby regains consciousness and starts to breathe normally.

Chapter 7: Crying and soothing

Nothing tugs at parents' heartstrings like the cries of their baby. The instinct to protect babies is very primal – so much so that the cries of various baby mammals are very similar and most mammals will even rush to the help of other mammals' babies if they are crying. It's an incredible bond between baby and parent and one that is important not to take lightly. If you leave a young baby crying you are breaking the very basic bond of seeking protection that the cry for help initiates. The impact of this in later life is a subject that's still being explored, but the suggestion is that it can have a profound impact on the bond between parent and child.

In this chapter we will help you with some of the more practical things you can do to soothe your crying baby, and look at ways you can even prevent some of that crying in the first place.

Why do babies cry?

First, try to keep in your mind that even if your baby seems really angry and upset, it's not directed at you, so don't take it personally. Your baby can't talk, so crying is his way of asking you to sort out a problem. Watch a midwife attending a crying baby, she will be very matter-of-fact and work through a list of all the reasons why he is crying one by one. Try to get into this mind-frame when your baby cries. Keep a 'list' in your head and work through it. Most of the time you'll sort it out and you'll soon get to know your baby's different cries. Below is the checklist that a midwife would work through. She will assess whether a baby:

- is hungry;
- is tired or overstimulated;

- is too hot or too cold;
- is unwell or in pain;
- has a dirty nappy;
- needs a cuddle.

How will I know if my baby is hungry?

To check whether your baby is hungry, stroke his cheek to see if he starts sucking or rooting for your finger, as if searching for your breast or the bottle. If he does, then he's hungry, so offer him a feed. Try not to get into the habit of giving your baby a dummy to stop him crying when he's hungry, as young babies especially need to be eating little and often. The same goes for encouraging thumb-sucking.

What if he's tired and overstimulated?

If your baby is overtired he may not look at you and will be very grumpy and will cry a lot. Although you know he needs sleep, he may have passed the point where he can drop off to sleep, especially if you are somewhere exciting. Take your baby to a calm and quiet room, soothe him and cuddle him to give him the chance to fall asleep. You'll soon start to recognise the signs that your baby is becoming overtired.

What if he's too hot or too cold?

He may be uncomfortable. Change his clothes or bedclothes; either wrap him up warmer if it's cold, or put him in lighter clothes if it's hot. A good tip is to remove labels inside the clothes, as these can be itchy or annoying for your baby.

How can I tell if he's unwell or in pain?

If your baby is unwell or in pain, his cry will be quite different from the usual tired/grumpy/wet nappy/hot/cold cry. You might be able to recognise this cry from when your baby has his immunisations – his cry will be very loud and sharp. It's impossible to ignore.

How often does he need his nappy changed?

Check to see if the nappy is dirty or wet. He can become uncomfortable quite quickly. Remember that babies need 'bare bum' time to keep their skin happy and prevent nappy rash (see pages 86-87).

How do I know if he just needs a cuddle?

All babies love to be carried and cuddled. If all of the other things in the 'crying list' haven't worked, this might be all your baby wants.

Can I prevent my baby from crying?

As you get to know your baby, you'll not only recognise his different cries, but more importantly you'll get to know when he tends to be hungry, sleepy, overtired and so on. As this happens you'll be able to anticipate these events and step in before he cries. You can feed him before he cries in hunger, you'll recognise the 'dirty-nappy face' before it turns into a sore-bottom/crying face, or put him down for a nap while he's still relaxed and before he is overtired.

Parents in many cultures carry their babies all the time and it's a great way to prevent your baby from crying. 'Baby wearing', as it's sometimes called, has been shown to make babies cry less. Both mums and dads can carry the baby around in a soft sling.

How can I soothe my crying baby?

To soothe your crying baby (and relax yourself) use these soothing techniques that parents have used all over the world for centuries:

- Walk about with him or rock him in a chair; the movement is soothing.
- Hold your baby in your arms close to your chest so he can feel your heartbeat.
- Use a gentle *Shhhhh* sounds – some doctors have suggested that this sound reminds babies of the calming 'white' noise in the womb. For the same reason, lots of babies love the white noise of a washing machine (or white noise tapes).
- Sing to your baby – a gentle lullaby is good – choose one that you sing all the time so he'll know it means time to calm down. You don't even need to remember the words – humming can be enough.
- Lots of babies will stop crying if you take them out for a walk in the pram, or even a drive in the car. It's up to you whether you decide to go down this route – you might not mind at all – but you might be creating a rod for your own back if this is the only way your baby will stop crying.

How can I cope when my baby cries a lot?
Babies have evolved to cry and parents have evolved to be upset by (and therefore respond to) that crying. So it is perfectly normal to become upset by your baby's crying. That said, it's exhausting for you to be going through the upset every day when you don't have to. A good trick is to pretend you're a midwife looking after your baby. Switch into professional mode, checking through the list of things above one by one. Most of the time this will sort it out. If this doesn't solve the problem there are other things you can do.

It is very upsetting, tiring and frustrating when a baby will not stop crying. Every parent feels overwhelmed at times, especially if they've not had a good night's sleep for weeks or even months. Ideally, speak to your friends or family and try to get some more help day to day. There are also support groups you can ring.

The most important thing to be aware of is that if you get to breaking point and you feel you are about to shake your baby, or something more violent, don't. Put your baby down somewhere safe, like his cot, and go to another room or outside until you feel calmer. Even if it takes you ten to 20 minutes to calm down and stop crying yourself, it is better for your baby if you do this rather than risk injuring him. Normally we would never suggest leaving a baby to cry on his own. We are suggesting this only as an alternative if you've reached the point of not being able to restrain yourself. If your baby is still crying when you go back to him, which he probably will be, then call a friend, your family or a helpline.

What is colic?

Lots of people use the generic term 'colic' to describe a baby who is tetchy and crying a lot more than babies usually do for no apparent reason. Many babies go through it. Your baby may pull her legs up to her tummy as if she is uncomfortable and arch her back when she's crying. She may cry most often in the late afternoon or evening. Health visitors, paediatricians and family doctors will often determine whether a baby has colic if her crying pattern follows the rule of threes: the colic-pattern crying started before she was three weeks old; she cries for more than three hours a day for at least three days of every week. Colic is not a modern problem; it happens all round the world and has been recorded frequently in history. Some paediatricians even think it's part of a baby's developmental process. Whatever happens, don't think it's your fault – babies with extremely relaxed, easy-going parents suffer from colic. The good news is that colic also starts to recede by the time a baby is three months old.

Should I take my colicky baby to see the doctor?
Yes, it's a good idea. If your baby is in pain, it's important to rule out any medical reasons for excessive crying, for example reflux (see page 107). It is also essential to rule out feeding problems, so make sure your baby is gaining weight and feeding is going well (see pages 130-133).

It is worth recording a video clip of your baby in the midst of the colic crying (as she's unlikely to do it at the doctors surgery) to show your doctor how distressing it is. Make a diary (how long after a feed does she start crying, what soothes your baby and so on) to discuss with the doctor. Take your partner with you, so you can both talk about how you feel. Your doctor can check that your baby is healthy and rule out some of the most common physical causes of excessive crying. Then at least you will know what you are dealing with.

It is extremely stressful, upsetting and exhausting trying to soothe a baby with colic. Your baby needs your support, but if you feel overwhelmed, frustrated and angry, it's really important to let someone else soothe the baby. It is safer to leave your baby in her cot if you are at the end of your tether. Never, never shake your baby. If you are finding it difficult, talk to your health visitor, doctor or other mums. You are not alone. Get lots of support during this tough time and try to remember that colic does go away after a couple of months.

Will massage help soothe a colicky baby?
If you've taken your baby to the doctor and you're reassured that she is otherwise well and healthy, then yes, it can help to massage your baby.

Firstly, make the room nice and warm, and warm up your hands. Undress your baby except for the nappy and lay her down on a firm, but soft surface such as thick rug, a mattress or a folded towel, ideally on the floor so there's no risk of falling. Here are a few moves that can help soothe a sore tummy.

Hand on tummy Simply place your warm hand gently and firmly over your baby's tummy. It can be very reassuring for her to know you understand where it's uncomfortable.

Warm flannel roll Take a warm, wet flannel and wring it out. Make it into a cylindrical shape and gently roll it up and down over your baby's tummy. The warmth is quite reassuring and relaxing for a baby.

Tummy massage With your baby lying on her back, feet towards you, massage her tummy with a simple clockwise movement. This can help to move any gas that's trapped in your baby's belly. It might produce some interesting noises!

Baby-bicycle move Hold your baby's ankles very gently, and fold her knees right up towards her tummy. Then start to rotate her knees around in a clockwise direction. The movement can really help to move any trapped wind, which you'll probably hear coming out, and your baby may be much happier.

Hand-over-hand massage Working from the top of the baby's tummy down to the top of her hips, gently stroke her tummy. Use the palm of your hand and alternate hands so there's always one in contact with your baby.

Rolling across your legs Sit down with your legs straight out in front of you, and lay your baby on her side across your thighs. Place your hand on her back, and gently roll her onto her tummy then over to her opposite side and back again. Gravity will do its job and put gentle pressure on your baby's tummy as it presses into your legs.

Sitting up hold This can only be used if you baby has good head control. Sit on the floor with your legs out in front of you. Sit your baby on your lap facing to one side. Press one hand gently against the small of her back, and apply gentle but firm pressure against her tummy with your other hand.

How do I know if my baby doesn't want a massage?

There are certain cues that babies give to let us know they're not happy to have a massage. If your baby doesn't make eye contact, is frowning and/or turning away or arching away, she is probably not enjoying it. You may have to wait until she is more receptive. Fussy babies sometimes don't like having their clothes taken off for a massage – so try leaving them on to see if that helps.

Should I offer my baby a dummy?

Dummies are very popular in many western countries – but almost unheard of in other parts of the world. If you do start using a dummy to help soothe your baby, remember you will have to wean him off it at a later date, which can be really hard. Babies will also drop dummies through the night, even if they're attached to the end of a ribbon, and won't go back to sleep until its found. There is research that suggests dummies can have positive effects as well. So read on below and you can decide.

Why should I not offer a dummy to a breastfeed baby?

Lactation experts tend to recommend that you should focus on establishing breastfeeding and making sure your baby learns that skill and is efficient at feeding at the breast before you even think about introducing a dummy. It takes a minimum of four weeks to become efficient at breastfeeding.

Will a dummy stop my baby crying if he's hungry?

If your baby is displaying feeding cues such as crying, trying to latch on, sucking strongly on anything (from your face to your finger), rooting and frantically searching for the breast or sucking his own fingers, he wants to be fed, so he should be free to express this. Feeding little and often is best for your baby. If you are breastfeeding, this signals to your body that it needs to make more breastmilk. Ignoring the signs and giving your baby a dummy instead of feeding him mean he may not get enough to eat and your milk supply can decrease. It's a vicious circle.

Do dummies cause potential physical problems?

Yes. Colic is more common in babies who use dummies, but research hasn't yet found out why this is. Tooth, bite and mouth development can be delayed if a baby uses a dummy beyond the age of six months.

Speech can also be delayed if a dummy is used too much and for too long; children simply won't or can't chat so much if there's something in their mouths. Babies with dummies tend to suffer more vomiting, fevers, diarrhoea and middle-ear infections. The middle-ear infections can increase as the sucking action may take bacteria from your baby's mouth into the narrow Eustachian tubes between his ears and throat. These infections can lead to fevers.

Can using dummies reduce the risk of SIDS. Is this true?
The Foundation for the Study of Infant Death, now called 'The Lullaby Trust', say that dummy use has been found to protect against SIDS, the reason for this is still unknown. It is thought to be because dummy-sucking increases blood pressure and heart rate during sleep.

Is it hard to wean a baby, toddler or child off a dummy?
Yes, which is another good reason not to start in the first place. Once a child has a dummy he may want it in his mouth all the time (not just for sleeping). It can be very stressful to wean a baby, toddler or child off a dummy. You can choose whether you make the baby go 'cold turkey' or whether you reduce its use gradually. We would always recommend the gentler techniques with babies. Remember it's not their fault; you gave them a dummy in the first place. If you do go for gradual withdrawal it is easier for both of you if you have a plan so it's easy for you to be consistent and for your child to accept the new rule. For example, start with having the dummy for naps and nights and then just nights.

Do dummies need to be sterilised?
If you do decide to use a dummy, make sure you follow these guidelines:

- Keep the dummy clean and sterilise it as you would a bottle teat.
- Flat orthodontic dummies are better for your baby's mouth development than rounded 'cherry-shaped' dummies.
- Offer the dummy for pain or settling, but don't let your baby have it all the time.
- Throw away dummies with cracks and holes as germs can lurk there.
- Try to wean your baby off the dummy by six months; it's much more difficult with an older baby or toddler.

Chapter 8: Development

The human brain is the most complex object in the known universe. A baby learns more in his first year of life than he will ever do again. He starts outs out as a tiny baby with very little control of his body, and by the end of the year he may well be on his feet and even uttering his first words. An adult brain will eventually have 100 billion brain cells, or neurons, and most of the connections between these cells are made the first year of life. In this chapter we look at how your baby will develop emotionally, socially and physically in this critical first year. We will provide insights into what you can do to nurture and encourage your developing baby.

Giving your baby a strong sense of attachment to you during his first two years will stand him in good stead for the rest of his life. The relationship a baby develops with his parents stimulates his brain and helps him to develop into a confident, independent and friendly adult. It is vital that you help to build and strengthen this bond.

Who checks my baby when she's born?

The midwife will give your newborn a thorough physical check. Your baby will be weighed and her head circumference and length will be measured. If your baby is born in hospital, she will be examined by a paediatrician (a doctor specialising in child health) before she is discharged. If she is born at home, your family doctor will carry out this assessment within 72 hours of the birth. The doctor will check her eyes, heart, hips, as well as all the natural reflexes that should be present at birth (see below). If you have a baby boy, the doctor will check to see if his testes have descended into the scrotum.

This initial assessment is to exclude the possibility of the most common physical abnormalities seen in newborn babies. If the paediatrician or doctor is concerned, your baby will be referred for specialist assessment in the hospital.

Are there any screening tests for newborns?

Yes, there are. All newborn babies have a routine hearing screening, known as an automated otoacoustic emission or AOAE test. This may be done before you leave the maternity unit, by your health visitor in your home, or at your doctor's surgery or health clinic. A small soft-tipped earpiece sends clicking sounds into your baby's ear. When the ear receives sound, the inner part, known as the cochlea, should produce an echo, which is picked up by the equipment.

Your newborn will also have a blood test (heel prick) when she is about five days old, which screens for the presence of a number of rare, but treatable conditions that could otherwise affect her development.

What developmental checks will my baby have as he grows?

When you are back at home, your health visitor will arrange for a developmental check at six to eight weeks with your doctor. Depending on your doctor's practice this is often timed to coincide with your baby's first immunisations, which are done at around eight weeks (see pages 102-103). He will have another developmental check with the health visitor when he's between nine months and one year.

What happens at a baby's first development check up?

At this assessment your baby will be weighed and his length and head circumference will be measured again. The doctor will listen to his heart again. Now that he is older, she will be able to hear if there is a heart murmur (extra or unusual sounds during a heartbeat) that might not have been apparent at birth. She will assess the hips again to rule out developmental dysplasia of the hip (also known as clicky hip), look at your baby's eyes for congenital cataracts, and again for boys she will check that the testes have descended into the scrotum. The doctor will look at your baby's muscle tone, spine, pulse in the femoral artery of the leg and assess for any hernias (such as a herniated umbilical cord). Your doctor may also ask how feeding is going and record whether your baby is being exclusively breastfed or formula-fed or a combination.

If your doctor has any concerns, your baby will be referred for further tests. For example, if your baby has a heart murmur he will be referred for an ultrasound to look at the structure and the blood flow in the heart. Some babies (especially premature babies) may have a tiny hole in the heart (a hole between the two ventricles, or lower chambers, of the heart), which can cause oxygenated and deoxygenated blood to mix. In many cases this hole will fuse naturally and no treatment will be necessary; in others surgery may be needed. Similarly if hip dysplasia is identified, an ultrasound of the hips may be done to decide if any treatment is required.

This check-up is also an opportunity for you to raise any matters of concern you have about your baby's development, health, feeding or weight gain. As a parent you have the best information about how your baby is doing and will be watching him more closely than anyone else so trust your instincts and double check anything you are worried about.

Will the doctor ask the parents any additional questions?
At the end of the six-week check your doctor will probably talk to you about parenting and baby health (especially as you may be having your six-week postnatal check at the same time). So expect discussions about contraception and smoking as well as nutrition, activity and accident prevention.

Is weight gain a prime indicator of overall health?

As a new parent there can seem to be a lot of focus on your baby's weight. Your baby will be weighed at birth, then your health visitor will give you a little red child health book, in which you and the health visitor can record your baby's weight gain over her first days, weeks, months and even years. It is good idea to have your baby weighed once a week until she is eight weeks old, once a month until she is six months old, then every other month until she is one year old.

If your baby is premature, born with a low birth weight or underlying health problem, or she has feeding issues, she will need to be assessed more frequently. This will depend on how premature she was, but the doctors in charge of her care will advise you. This can be very stressful for you as a parent, especially if your baby doesn't put on as much weight as your health visitor would like. Sometimes healthcare professionals will use upsetting medical phrases like 'failure to thrive' and parents often report feeling as if they have failed. Even the common phrases like 'she's a big, bouncing baby' can reinforce this feeling.

Can babies put on too much weight?
Young babies are supposed to put on a lot of weight and have good fat deposits as they are growing at a faster rate than they ever will for the rest of their lives. Interestingly, there has been a lot of new research looking at the effects of high rates of weight gain and baby weight. Scientists are now reporting that very big babies and babies with a high rate of weight gain may actually face more long-term health problems, such as high blood pressure and diabetes in adulthood, than babies who put on an average amount of weight. So the medical profession looks at optimum weight gain, which can be observed in breastfed babies that are feeding well. If your formula-fed baby is up in the highest percentile of weight for her age then it's worth checking with doctor and/or health visitor whether she is gaining weight too quickly. Certainly if your baby is above the healthy weight limit, you should discuss this with your doctor and/or health visitor. A breastfed baby is unlikely to be above the recommended weight limits.

What is the optimal weight gain?
What seems to be important is that you watch for and respond to your baby's feeding cues (signals of hunger and fullness) as she feeds and grows. Feed her when she's hungry and let her stop when she has had enough. Formula-fed babies should not be 'forced' to finish a bottle of

milk; parents should be led by their baby's signals – not the amount of milk left in the bottle. This sensitive feeding style is also encouraged during weaning as the medical profession is seeing more and more very young children who are already seriously overweight, even obese. If you are concerned about your baby's weight, weight gain or feeding behaviour, talk to your doctor or health visitor.

What do the weight charts show?
The weight charts in your red book map your baby's weight and weight gain and compare it to other babies of the same sex and age. Since 2006, the World Health Organisation (WHO) baby weight charts are based on breastfed boy babies or girl babies from around the world. In the past, doctors may have used growth charts based on white babies and included formula-fed babies who do not always put on weight in the optimal pattern observed in breastfed babies who are feeding successfully.

When your baby is weighed, the result will be recorded on a graph with her age along one axis and weight on the other. Your baby's weights are shown on the chart in percentiles, or centiles, so you can see how your baby is progressing and how she compares to her peers. If your daughter's weight at one month is on the 35th percentile, this means that if there were 100 one-month old baby girls together in a room, 34 would weigh less than your baby and 65 would weigh more.

Your health visitor will also be interested to see whether your baby's weight continues along the same percentile. Generally if your baby's weight when she was born was on the 35th percentile or the 70th percentile, for example, you would hope to see her stay around that level (excepting for growth spurts and little dips) during her first year.

If your doctor or health visitor sees a consistent fall in the weight gain against the growth percentile, your baby may be referred to a paediatrician. Likewise if there is a feeding problem she may be assessed by an infant feeding expert to check that there are no medical or anatomical (for example, tongue tie: see pages 21-22) reasons for the low weight gain. Medics may use the term 'failure to thrive', which can be upsetting, but if there is an underlying problem, the sooner it can be identified, the quicker they can help your baby and hopefully she will start to put on weight again and track along her percentile.

What are the key developmental milestones?

A newborn baby has a lot to learn. When you see a newborn foal, it's up on its, admittedly wobbly, feet almost immediately. By contrast, a human baby is almost completely helpless and it may be around a year before he can walk. This is largely because humans are born 'prematurely' before their brains are fully developed, to make birth safer for them and their mothers.

The human brain is one of the most complex objects, and in the first two years it will triple in weight. Your baby's brain has to learn a vast array of physical and mental skills all at the same time. He has to learn seemingly 'simple' physical tasks like controlling his head, turning it, sitting up, rolling over, crawling, coordinating pincer movement between fingers and thumbs, and getting up to walk. Alongside this your baby has to learn to communicate, speak, see, and bond with his parents, and a lot more social, emotional and cognitive developments.

Your baby will learn faster and develop and change more than he will ever do again in his first year. However, every baby is different, so don't worry if yours doesn't meet all these milestones exactly as described here; look at the ranges of ages instead. If you have concerns, talk to your doctor or health visitor. If necessary he or she can have your baby assessed, as early intervention is really important if your baby has any developmental delays. Remember, all the ages mentioned below will be later for premature babies who'll need longer to get their strength. Use their due date as guide, although in reality it's likely to be somewhere between the birth date and due date.

Central and fundamental to all baby development is your baby's attachment to you. The most important thing for your baby's social and emotional development in his first two years is how he 'attaches' to you, and how you 'attach' to him. You can help your child along by talking to him, singing, listening, lots of cuddling, and lots of skin-to-skin contact. The more love you can pour into your little baby in those first vital years, the stronger and more independent he will be when he grows up.

Birth

Physical ability A newborn baby has very little control of his body, but will probably be able to wriggle his arms and legs on both sides of his body equally well.

His grasp reflex is present, along with the startle (or Moro) reflex, the rooting reflex (instinctive urge to breastfeed), and the stepping reflex (where if you hold your baby upright he will try to step).

Your baby can see from birth, but he can only see clearly around 30 cm (1 ft): the perfect distance to mum's face when he's being held. This is called 'fixing'. His hearing should be fully developed at birth. If your baby doesn't respond to a sudden loud noise like a clap or a bell, mention this to your doctor.

Cognitive ability Your baby will already know your voice from his time in your womb, and will prefer your voice to all others.

Emotional ability Your baby will love making eye contact with you and looking at your face. He will also love copying you. Encourage this by playing the sticking-out-your-tongue game: if you stick your tongue out, he might do the same. This is your very first 'conversation'.

Month 1

Physical development Your baby may be able to lift his head briefly when lying on his front. Within a few days after birth your baby can turn to a big light source like a window, and close his eyes to a sudden bright light. His eyes will be drawn to moving objects. He can still only focus around 30 cm (1 ft).

Cognitive development He may be developing a preference for familiar sounds and objects, like your face and voice. Talk to your baby all the time and give him time to gurgle in response.

Emotional development He may start to smile back at you when you smile at him (and it will be the best feeling in the world).

Month 2

Physical development By six to eight weeks your baby can probably move his gaze slowly and follow an object moving slowly from side to side at a distance of about 15 cm (6 inches). This is called 'following'. He may be able to lift his head briefly when lying on his tummy.

Cognitive development Your baby will recognise you, but at six weeks he doesn't demonstrate a reaction when you leave him. He doesn't yet hold the concept of 'mum' in his head when he's alone (even though he recognises your face, smell and voice and prefers them to others). He's probably not frightened of strangers.

Emotional development Your baby may probably smile in response to your smile and will be beginning to make little cooing noises; give him lots of smiles and talk to him to encourage this. He will probably respond in some way by now if you ring a little bell – either by looking startled, upset or going quiet.

Month 3

Physical development Your baby can probably lift his head and possibly shoulders off the floor if he lies on his front. He can probably bring his hands together.

Cognitive development He plays with, and continues to discover his own hands, arms, feet and legs and the sensation as they make contact with other things.

Emotional development He may squeal with delight at things by now, and be starting to develop a hearty laugh. He will probably be aware of object permanence from three months; in other words he expects things that disappear behind a wall to return. If you start by partially covering an object, then he'll come to understand that the object is there even when it's completely covered up.

Month 4

Physical development His controlled grasp begins to develop. When he's offered a rattle he may reach for it. Allow time when you hold out an object since he is still developing his hand-eye coordination.

Cognitive development More intention will probably become apparent in your baby's behaviour. There may be signs of him understanding object permanence. He may look or reach for an object that is partly hidden from view (as he understands that it is still there) and he really begins to enjoy peek-a-boo. He also understands person permanence (mum or dad) and is not surprised when you return.

Emotional development He may laugh with full eye contact, and be turning his head towards you when he hears your voice.

Month 5

Physical development He will probably have good head control. He can raise his body with his arms if he's lying on his front. He can roll over in one direction and he can reach for things to grab.

Cognitive development He will probably be experimenting with vowel sounds by now and putting interesting combinations of sounds together. From five months he might be very curious if he can see multiple reflections of you at the same time as he knows by now that there is only one of you.

Emotional development He might start objecting to things by this age. For example, he may become annoyed if you take something away that he wants, like a toy. He will probably start trying to get things for himself, such as reaching for food he likes the look of.

Month 6

Physical development Your baby will probably be able to sit up (supported initially) between five and nine months. He may hold his head level and steady if you hold his hands when he's lying down and gently pull his up into a sitting position.

Cognitive development He explores objects by putting them in his mouth. If he drops something and it disappears he might start looking for it.

Emotional development Your baby will babble by himself by controlling his voice box (he'll say baa baa, daa daa) but probably won't have any words.

Month 7

Physical development He can probably sit without support. He has enough coordination to be able to put finger foods in his mouth. He will probably be able to bear some weight on his legs if held up. He may begin crawling or moving on all fours (classic), on his bottom (shuffling), on his tummy (commando) or even sideways (the crab). This may begin at six months, but it's usually between seven and eight months. Allow safe space and time to practice. Some babies don't crawl at all; they just get up and walk later.

Cognitive development He may have an increasing sense of things being near and far away from him. He might start calling you (both) Mamma and Dadda.

Emotional development He loves to squeal and smile and interact with you.

Month 8

Physical development Your baby can probably now pass a small toy from one hand to the other and back again. Cruising on furniture may have started.

Cognitive development He now probably understands object permanence fully and will look for an object that is completely hidden from view. He may be beginning to understand cause-and-effect play, and will enjoy and notice that his physical actions result in noises and movement of other objects. Peek-a-boo games are great at this stage.

Emotional development Separation anxiety may begin and he will cry when he can't see you. This can start as early as six months but tends to peak at ten months and recede by the time he is two.

Month 9

Physical development Your baby may start trying to move towards a toy that's out of reach. He might be trying to practice cruising – but don't worry at all if he hasn't yet.

Cognitive development Cause and effect is developing and he may begin to enjoy stacking cups and then watching them fall over.

Emotional development Separation anxiety continues. He starts to notice the tone of your voice more than your words.

Month 10

Physical development Fine motor control begins and your baby may be able to pick up little objects with his thumb and forefinger. He is not yet left- or right-handed. He may stand holding on to someone or something.

Cognitive development Your baby will love looking at picture books. He may help you turn the pages; he might even want to kiss or bite the pages. A baby may begin to use body language such as shaking his head.

Emotional development He may have a have a couple of words; for example, 'Bye bye'.

Month 11

Physical development Your baby may now move into a sitting position from lying on his tummy.

Cognitive development He may notice when you say 'No', for example if you want him to stop doing something dangerous, but he won't necessarily stop doing it. He might be able to say a few words other than Mamma or Dadda.

Emotional development You baby might also be able to distinguish between saying Mamma and Dadda by now.

Month 12

Physical development Your baby may start walking by holding on to furniture or you. On average this begins around his first birthday but it can happen as early as nine months, or as late as 18 months.

Cognitive development Your baby can probably retrieve a hidden object more than once, but does not look for objects that are completely out of his field of perception. He might be able to follow a simple command like 'Give that to me, please' with your arm held out. He might be able to wave hello or bye bye. He might be able to roll a ball back to you.

Emotional development He will start to communicate using pointing.

What if my baby is premature?

Premature babies generally develop more slowly than their peers born at full term. It's a good idea in general with premature babies to measure their development from their expected birth date, rather than their actual birth date, although they tend to reach milestones somewhere between the two dates. If your baby was born very prematurely she may face long-term difficulties with her development and you may need more support and advice from your local child-development team. You should also discuss with your baby's paediatric team what to expect with your baby's development and if they expect any long-term development issues.

The one golden rule for all new babies would be to 'encourage' your baby – don't 'force' her. You cannot speed up your baby's development by a kind of 'bootcamp' approach. Babies learn best in a sensitive, warm and relaxed environment. There's a complicated series of physical developments that need to coordinate alongside brain developments – it's like a feedback loop. If you try to push her before she's ready, you will frustrate her, rather than help her. So, let your baby guide you as to whether she's happy learning new things.

Why is it so important that I should bond with my baby?

If you compare a newborn human baby to most other mammal babies, you'll notice a huge difference. The amount of time a human baby needs for its very large brain to develop means that he's very vulnerable – particularly for the first two years – and is reliant on his parents. For this reason all babies need to form what psychologists call a 'secure attachment' with their mum and/or dad (or their primary care-giver).

There is a great deal of scientific evidence to show that the quality of this bond is reflected in how a child develops. A good secure bond in the early years helps him become a resilient, happy and independent adult. It's an enormous responsibility, but it's one that can be achieved very enjoyably if you know a few of the guidelines.

How do hormones help bonding?

Initial bonding at the birth and soon afterwards may develop almost automatically. Mums start producing the hormone oxytocin during pregnancy, but levels increase in the later stages of pregnancy and peak during birth. Oxytocin promotes love, bonding and calmness and reduces fear. Breastfeeding triggers more oxytocin to be released but so does cuddling your baby. If you're bottle-feeding, have lots of skin-to-skin contact and look into your baby's eyes and cuddle him as this will also release oxytocin to promote your bond with each other.

The human body and its hormones are quite remarkable. Parents may even produce oxytocin in the run-up to adopting a child and when they are first united with their new baby or child will fall in love and bond in the same way.

What if I don't feel the bond at the birth?

Bonding with your baby is a process, not a one-off event. Some parents have the 'movie-moment' at the birth, where they fall madly in love with their baby at first sight. This is wonderful, but it very often doesn't happen, particularly if you've had a traumatic birth, an epidural or a Caesarean delivery. You could well feel quite distant from everything at the moment of birth. Don't worry – there is a great deal you can do to make sure you lose nothing of the bond with your baby. Lots of parents get to know their baby slowly and feel a bond developing each hour and each day. Some parents may take even longer.

Even if you don't feel the bond and the love straightaway, your baby will still love you. Try to give him as much skin-to-skin contact as you can to promote the release of oxytocin and start a feedback loop even if you don't feel the bond at the start. Breastfeeding also helps this process, but it's released during bottle-feeding too (see page 30). Try carrying your baby in a sling as much as you can – he'll love hearing your breathing sounds and heartbeat as well as feeling the warmth of your skin. Above all, try not to worry.

BONDING AFTER A CAESAREAN BIRTH?
If you have a planned Caesarean, ask for your baby to be placed on your chest after the birth. Discuss the possibility of a small delay in the cutting of the cord. Skin-to-skin contact straight after birth is enormously helpful for bonding; even if you're feeling dreadful, your baby will love it. If the team will let you, try a first feed of colostrum as soon as possible after the birth; this can help start the bonding process. It is also possible to do this after an emergency Caesarean, provided you are conscious. If you are not, ask to cuddle the baby as soon as possible afterwards.

How can dads bond?
Skin-to-skin contact works just as well with dads as it does with mums. A dad can unbutton his shirt and your baby will love lying on his chest, listening to his heartbeat and feeling his warmth. Dads also produce oxytocin when they cuddle their babies, which helps them to bond, feel calm and helps the babies feel secure.

Is it more difficult to bond with twins?
The amount of work involved with twins can mean that time for 'bonding' can fall by the wayside initially. Many parents of twins say they found it much harder (or slower) to bond with multiple babies than singletons.

Some parents bond equally well with both babies, but many find that they bond better with one of the twins, and often feel guilty about it. It's actually very normal, but most parents won't talk about it since they might feel worried about it or even ashamed. Try to be aware of this if you can; be proactive and spend the same amount of time with each baby. You may even find the stronger bond you feel shifts from one baby to the other(s) at times. Try to be objective and give each baby the same obvious love and care. Every baby is different – some will be easy-going and sleep well – others will be fractious, colicky and irritable. Early personality traits can make it much easier to bond with one baby and not another, but every baby needs your love equally. If you're bonding less with one baby, try to spend more time with that baby, and ask your partner (or a friend) to help with the other one. Sometimes just a few days of undivided attention and love will make a big difference and you'll find you start to develop a bond. Also try to spend time with each baby on his own.

What does not vary is that families with twins (or multiples) find that the feeling of exhaustion is even higher than with a single baby. This might mean that the amount of time you have to spend just cuddling or playing might be much lower. You will be spending all your time feeding, bathing, changing nappies, and trying to feed yourself and catch up on your own sleep as well.

The most important thing to remember is that bonding doesn't have to be instantaneous – and in fact it rarely is. Bonding may come immediately, soon after the birth, months later, or can even develop very slowly over the years. As long as you are there for your babies, love them as best you can, and give them all the time and attention you can, then the bond will develop. If you really feel you're having deeper trouble, seek help quickly. Lots of other people have been through what you're going through and it's important to get support.

How can I encourage my baby's mobility?

It's hugely important – way before your baby can walk – to play with her out of her pram or bouncy chair for a good amount of time every day. She will take longer to improve her mobility if you don't do this. Encourage your baby to move as much as possible, at whatever stage she's at. She needs to learn lots of skills before she can get up onto her feet and there are lots of things you can do to help her.

How does tummy time help?

The first thing you can help with is strengthening your baby's back muscles. You can do this with what's called 'tummy time' as soon as your baby shows signs of being able to lift her head. You can simply lay your baby on her tummy somewhere firm and soft (like a firm mattress with no duvet on it), and she will practice lifting her head and may even arch her back up too.

You can all play together too. Sit on the floor opposite someone else and bend your knees slightly. Lay your baby on her tummy along your thighs (feet towards you), with her head just above your knees. The person opposite can encourage your baby to look up. When your baby needs a rest, she can drop her head back down on your knees. You can give her a gentle back massage while she's lying on your legs too.

How can I teach her to roll?

By around five months most babies can roll over, but they might start from around three months. You can encourage your baby by giving her lots of time to practice. Lay her on a rug and place a small toy just out of reach, so that she has to roll over to get it. Remember to give her lots of encouragement and praise as she tries to reach it.

Should I help crawling?

Crawling is quite complex and requires a lot of brain development and coordination. Babies crawl (or start moving around) in all sorts of funny ways – it might be the classic crawl on all fours, or on one knee and one foot. Some opt to move commando-style on their tummies and others shuffle along on their bottoms. This locomotion can happen between the ages of six to ten months. Learning to crawl can take a while to coordinate, so give your baby lots of time on a good safe surface like a clean carpet or rug or grass in the park. In the same way as you encouraged rolling, put a favourite toy a small distance away so she needs to crawl to get it.

If your baby is crawling sideways, it's usually fine, but note that if she always favours one side, it might indicate other problems so it's important to have this checked by your doctor or health visitor.

My baby wants to stand up all the time. Is this OK?

Some babies want to stand from a very young age. Let her stand on your lap and bounce up and down as this can strengthen her knees and feet. The main point is not to force her – never use a walking machine. Let your baby develop at her own pace.

What is cruising?

Cruising means walking by holding on to things like sofas, chairs or mum and dad and may start at about nine months – but it's often much later, so do not fret. This is the last stage before your baby will get up and walk on her own. A baby's duck-like gait, the lack of a foot arch and underdeveloped balance make early walking really difficult for her. You can help your baby along by providing a series of big chairs or sofas that she can hold on to as she tries to move around the room. Your baby will probably start by working out how to bend her knees and how to sit after standing. If your baby has not started cruising by around 18 months, it is worth getting her checked out by your health visitor, as almost all children are walking by this age.

How can I help my baby practice cruising and walking?

Step one is to encourage your baby to squat down from a standing position by placing something interesting on the floor that she has to squat down to grab. At first, she may just fall down on the floor as she tries to reach the toy, but after a while she will be able to squat down and pick up the toy, then stand up again. All this pulling to stand, squatting up and down, and cruising from side to side helps your baby develop the strength, balance, and coordination necessary for walking.

Once your baby is interested in trying to cruise, help her to practice walking by holding both her hands and letting her 'walk' in front of you. Holding hands like this stimulates development of the part of her brain that controls balance and coordination; it's like a feedback loop. When she's ready, drop down to one hand.

You can also help her by propping her up next to the sofa so she's in the right start position and can move along the sofa on her own. If she's sitting near the sofa, place one of her favourite toys on the edge, to encourage her to pull herself up against the sofa. Once she's up, move the toy along the sofa a little so she edges along to get it. Never force your child if she's not ready.

Should I buy my baby a walking device?

A tiny pushchair or push-along trolley is a good idea. A baby still has to get up on her own and move on her own, but the pushchair is like a tiny zimmer frame that gives her some extra support without taking control of her.

Don't use the 'baby walkers' where the baby sits in a harness and rolls around pushing with her legs. These aren't good for a baby's development. A baby needs to learn to cruise slowly, building up her brain development and coordination in tandem with her strength.

Should I encourage my baby to walk?

Don't push things is the golden rule. Lots of holding both hands, then one hand, is the best thing to encourage walking. Give her as much time to practice as you can – out in the park or at home on the carpet. Most babies are walking by about a year, but babies can walk as early as nine months and others wait until they are 18 months. If your baby is 18 months and is still not walking, you should talk to your doctor. If your baby tends to favour one side of her body tell your doctor too as it may indicate a weakness along one side.

Should my baby wear shoes or are bare feet okay?

Practice cruising or walking at home or in the park just in bare feet, non-slip socks or soft leather shoes so her feet will learn all the little movements needed to balance. You can get your baby her first pair of shoes when she is walking confidentially, and even then only for when she is walking outside. Keep your baby in bare feet or non-slip socks as long as possible and as much as possible since it helps her learn how to balance, and lets her feet develop naturally without any restrictions. When you do get your baby's first shoes, go to a children's shoe shop and have the experienced fitter look at your baby's feet, measure them properly and advise you on the right type of shoes.

How can I encourage my baby's fine motor skills?

The ability to pick objects up with our thumb and forefinger is what separates humans from other animals. This ability is the basis for nearly everything we do, such as writing and holding a knife and fork. We are not born with is this skill, and it takes a baby a while to develop it.

Your baby starts by grasping on to big objects with his whole hand, then gradually develops the ability to hold smaller things, until he can carefully pick items up between his thumb and forefinger alone. As with all other skills this ability develops later in premature babies.

Why can he grasp at birth?
You might think your baby is amazingly developed because at birth he can already grasp your thumb. This is actually what's known as his 'grasp reflex'. He is born with this ability but it isn't under his control – even though it feels like it is. Between the age of three and five months, your baby will start to control his grasp. To start with he'll use his whole hand. Encourage him by offering bright-coloured objects that are easy to hold. Put toys within easy reach and let him pick them up one by one and play with them.

How does he learn the thumb and forefinger grip?
Sometime between the age of six months and 11 months, your baby will occasionally be picking up smaller things between his thumb and forefinger. He'll get it right sometimes and drop it other times. He's practising and it's good to encourage development by offering small things like raisins or bits of apple, which have the added bonus of being a sweet reward. Your baby probably won't master this skill until he's about 15 months old.

When will my baby start clapping and waving?
By around nine to 13 months, your baby might be starting to clap and wave. You can encourage him by clapping his hands together for him, so he'll feel and see what it's like. Then try clapping in front of him. He has a natural instinct to copy your actions. If you clap, he'll clap; wave at him and he'll do the same. As your baby becomes more coordinated, try playing clapping games.

Why does my baby want to knock things over and drop them?
Knocking things over and dropping things is an important step in his development; he's not being naughty. In fact, you should actively encourage him to do it as he's learning about cause and effect. It does

not need to be toys; try getting some cereal boxes and build towers that he can knock down; he will love it. Or give him objects that he can drop into a box and make a big noise. Doing this outside in the dirt has the added bonus of being good for developing his immune system too. Your baby probably won't start putting things together (rather than knocking them down) until he's about 18 months old.

Can I tell whether my baby is going to be left- or right-handed?
No. Most babies are completely ambidextrous until they are around 18 months old, when they start to favour one hand. Let your baby lead you in this – don't try to force anything to change that isn't natural. If your baby favours one hand earlier than this, it's a good idea to tell your health visitor or doctor as they may want to assess him further.

How can I help my baby communicate and talk?

You'd be expecting your baby to be starting with a few words by the time she reaches the age of one year, but her brain will have been absorbing information long before she can talk. You can, and should, do a huge amount of communication with her before she can actually talk. The best encouragement you can give her is really very simple – paying her lots of attention, smiling and laughing with her, talking to her a lot, and giving her time to 'respond' to you with her gurgling and babbling. By doing this, you'll be laying the ground for a communicative and attentive child, who will enjoy talking, listening and feeling included and loved.

When do babies start babbling?
Your baby will start babbling to herself, her toys, even you, at around five to seven months. 'Da' is often one of the first sounds – which dads always love and mums sometimes feel upset by. Don't be. It's just an easier sound to make than 'ma'! Interestingly, the way that babies babble is the same all over the world. Whether you're in London or Lima, young babies sound the same.

How do I encourage my baby to talk?

Before your baby can start joining in the conversation, a nice thing to do is chat to her about what's happening. Let her hear your voice: 'Look at the beautiful blue sky today' or 'Isn't it cold? Let's put our coats on before we go out…'. She will also be getting very familiar with the language you speak by hearing lots of words over and over again.

When you're talking to your baby, give her the opportunity to 'respond' too. She will think she's saying something too and she'll enjoy the whole process a lot. You'll probably be surprised how much she babbles away if you let her. Your baby also will feel valued and loved if you talk to her and include her all the time – this not only helps language, it's a hugely important part of the ongoing bonding process.

What is baby talk or 'Motherese'?

'Motherese' or 'Mother Ease' or 'parentese' are terms for the special voice that parents sometime use to speak to their babies. Dads can use it too. It's a sing-song, cooing voice – a bit like the voice we use with cute pets.

What is baby signing?

Baby signing is a form of pre-verbal communication that builds on the fact that babies understand so much before they can talk. Lots of people like the idea of using hand signs for simple words with their baby – like a sign for 'milk', for example. Baby signing is a whole subject on its own which we don't have space to go into here, but we'd encourage you to learn more about it and try it for yourself. If you want to find out more, research courses in your area.

How do babies learn language?

As babies develop, they stop their universal babble and tune in to the particular language that is being spoken around them. Babies can learn more than one language fairly easily. It becomes much harder to learn another language by around the age of seven. If you speak two or three languages, don't be afraid to use them all. A good tip is for one parent to speak one language, the other parent to speak another – and maybe Grandma to speak a third. Having different people speaking the languages helps avoid confusion. It might be that the baby will take longer to speak clearly in two or three languages than she would if she were learning just one, but that is natural when there's so much more she's learning. It's such an enormous advantage for a child growing up that it's worth spending time on it if when she's little. However, if you are speaking more than one language to your child and she is still not speaking clearly by the age of three, get her assessed to make sure he does not have a hearing problem like glue ear (see page 150).

How do I know if my baby has hearing problems?

Hearing screening is usually done just after the birth in hospital – or soon after in your home (see page 129). This initial screening picks up most hearing problems in young babies.

If initial screening does not show a clear response from both ears, your baby will need a second test. This is quite common, and this doesn't necessarily mean that your baby has hearing loss. Your baby may have been unsettled, there may have been some background noise or your baby may have had fluid in his ear from the birth. The second screening may be the same as the first one or if not, your baby may be given an Automated Auditory Brainstem Response (AABR) screening test, which involves three small sensors being placed on your baby's head and neck. If a problem is found you will be referred for further investigation by an audiologist. There are many treatments for children with mild to severe hearing impairment from surgery to hearing aids. The specialist can advise you of the relevant options.

Your baby should respond to a loud unexpected noise like a door banging. A young baby would respond by looking startled, perhaps, or just taking notice. You would expect an older baby with head control to turn towards the sound.

If a young baby doesn't startle or take notice of a sudden loud noise or if an older baby (with head control) doesn't turn towards it, talk to your doctor health visitor. Your doctor may refer your baby for a hearing test. You can also self-refer your baby for a hearing test via your health visitor.

What is glue ear?

Glue ear is the most common cause of hearing loss in children and it's important to get it treated quickly. Glue ear occurs when the tubes between the nose and the ear (Eustachian tubes) become blocked with mucus so that fluid accumulates against the eardrum. As a result the baby cannot hear very well because the tiny bones in the ear can't vibrate as they should. If your baby seems to be having trouble hearing, isn't responding as usual, is having problems sleeping, ear pain and balance or clumsiness problems, then go and talk to your doctor. If he suspects glue ear he may refer your child for a hearing test. However, most cases of glue ear resolve without intervention. Your doctor may recommend decongestants to help clear the tubes. If the hearing difficulty persists your child will be referred to the local ear, nose and throat (ENT) department for further assessment and treatment. Some children need grommets (minute tubes) inserted into the eardrum during surgery.

It's really important to get your baby or child's hearing checked if you suspect glue ear. If treated successfully there shouldn't be any long-term effects. If glue ear is not treated, it can impair hearing and lead to speech and language delay.

How does a baby's vision develop?

Babies are not born with perfect vision and there are several developmental steps they need to go through. A newborn baby's eyesight is quite blurry, but she can focus over a fixed distance of around 30 cm (1 ft). This is perfect for her as it's the distance from her mum's breast to her mum's face. In the first few days watch to see if your baby is:

- turning her eyes towards a big light source – like a window when the blind is opened;
- closing her eyes to sudden bright light;
- being drawn to moving objects, such as your face.

When can she start to see further?

The ability to focus on one thing, like your face, is known as fixing. Babies can do this quite early on. As your baby grows, she should be able to track slow side-to-side movements of nearby objects, like a dangling toy, or your face. This is called following.

You can introduce games that help your baby's eyesight develop. To help her practice fixing and following, try holding a favourite toy (black, white and red are good colours and face designs are very popular with babies) at the magic 30 cm (1 ft) from her face. When you have her attention, move it very slowly left and right so that she can follow it with her eyes. If by about six weeks of age you don't think your baby is fixing and following, then you should talk to your doctor or health visitor.

What should I do if she has crossed eyes or a squint?

Newborn baby's eyes often looked cross-eyed or squinty, but if it seems to be happening all the time, or if she seems to have difficulty moving her eyes in one direction, it's worth checking with your health visitor or doctor.

Will a premature baby's eyesight be different?

Your baby's eyes only finish developing at the end of pregnancy so babies who arrive early may have less control of their eyes than a full-term baby. This is quite normal and you would expect vision to strengthen as a baby approaches her expected birth date. However, if she is premature or 'small for dates' she will be assessed for 'retinopathy of prematurity', which is caused by not having fully developed blood vessels to the retina (the back of the eye that receives light and sends messages to the brain about colour, contrast and movement in the environment). Retinopathy of prematurity is treatable if screened and spotted.

What do I do if I think something is wrong?

Most baby's physical and cognitive development follows the same pattern and stages. Sometimes, however, they don't – for example, some babies walk without ever crawling. It is important to remember, though that each baby will reach his developmental milestones at very different times. Some will talk quickly but walk slowly; others will be up and about well before their peers but talk much later than their friends. As a parent it is impossible not to compare your baby to the other babies you know. This can be a helpful yardstick and most babies do end up hitting all their developmental milestones sooner or later (See pages 133-138 for a guide to your baby's developmental milestones).

However, it is important not to be too complacent or hide your anxiety if you are really worried about your baby's development. You know your baby best and see how your baby changes, responds and develops day in day. This is the kind of information that a doctor can never hope to absorb during a short appointment. You are very much the advocate for your essentially helpless baby. If you do think that your baby is very different from his peers, you should speak to your doctor or health visitor. It can sometimes help to video anything that you think helps to illustrate your baby's problem. For example, if your baby drags his leg or only uses one hand to pick things up, try to film it on your phone, then show the video to your doctor.

If your baby's doctor or health visitor shares your concern they will assess the baby first and then refer him for an initial assessment by your local child development team (who include paediatricians, speech and language therapists). For example, if you feel he is not responding normally to noises, he may have glue ear. This can have implications on his language development so insist on a hearing test.

A good doctor or health visitor will always listen to the concerns of a parent. It can also help to contact a support group as it can often be very knowledgeable and either put your mind at rest or recommend further assessment for your baby (see resources, page 160). It is important to see your doctor if you are concerned about delays in your baby's development. He or she may well be able to reassure you that there isn't a problem. It's best to get your baby assessed medically by your doctor or even referred to your child-development team, since it can, on rare occasions, be a sign of something being wrong. The good news is that with early intervention, many problems can be resolved or your baby will be offered community support to help promote his development.

Index

Acknowledgements

We would like to thank the following organisations for their guidance and expert advice:

Child Accident Prevention Trust (CAPT)

www.capt.org.uk
The Child Accident Prevention Trust (CAPT) is the UK's leading charity working to reduce the number of children and young people killed, disabled or seriously injured in accidents.

Meningitis Research Foundation

www.meningitis.org
This foundation researches into the prevention, detection and treatment of meningitis and to share knowledge gained by research so everyone can benefit.

National Literacy Trust

www.literacytrust.org.uk
The National Literacy Trust is a national charity dedicated to raising literacy levels in the UK.

Royal College of Paediatrics and Child Health (RCPCH)

www.rcpch.ac.uk
The RCPCH mission is to transform child health through knowledge, innovation and expertise. The Essential Parent Company provides video clips to the RCPCH. These are used to help train junior paediatricians in the UK and abroad.

St John Ambulance

www.sja.org.uk
St John Ambulance is the nation's leading first-aid charity. Every year, more than 800,000 people learn how to save a life through their training programmes.

UNICEF UK Baby Friendly Initiative

www.unicef.org.uk/babyfriendly/
The UK Baby Friendly Initiative is based on a global accreditation programme of UNICEF and the World Health Organization. It is designed to support breastfeeding and parent/infant relationships by working with public services to improve standards of care.

We would also like to thank the following experts who have generously donated their time and expertise to help us.

Mandy Gurney, Director of the Millpond Sleep Clinic

www.millpondsleepclinic.com
The Essential Parent Company's sleeping expert is Mandy Gurney. Millpond is the longest-established private sleep clinic in the UK and the only one to offer sleep training for children, from babies through to adolescence.

Dr Deborah Hodes, Consultant Community Paediatrician

Dr Deborah Hodes works in the community trust for the London Borough of Camden and at University College London Hospitals. She has led the work that The Essential Parent Company and the RCPCH have done together.

Melissa Little, Paediatric Dietitian and Baby Nutrition Expert

Melissa Little is a practising member of the Freelance Dietitian's Group and Paediatric Group and is fully registered with the Health Professionals Council and the British Dietetic Association.

Alice MacLaine, Nursery Teacher
Alice Maclaine is a Montessori trained nursery teacher at the prestigious Rolfe's Nursery School in Notting Hill, London.

Dr Anna Maw BSc MBBS MRCPCH
Dr Anna Maw is a consultant paediatrician at Cambridge University NHS Trust. She specialises in brain development and neurology.

Alison Ross, Registered Midwife, DipHe, BSc (Hons)
Alison Ross was a specialist midwife for mental health at Kingston Hospital. As well as all the practical skills of looking after a new baby, she was specially trained in supporting new mums who are feeling overwhelmed, sad and depressed.

Sally Tedstone, Midwife and Breastfeeding Educator, UNICEF UK Baby Friendly Initiative
Sally Tedstone is The Essential Parent Company's supportive breastfeeding expert with a wealth of practical experience of helping mums learn to breastfeed, as well as a strong understanding of how breastfeeding works.

Dr Sarah Temple MBBChir MRCGP DRCOG
www.ehcap.co.uk/dr-sarah-temple
Dr Sarah Temple is The Essential Parent Company's expert children's GP. She is working as a portfolio NHS GP in Somerset. With more than 20 years' experience working with children and young people, both within general practice and mental health services, Sarah has a special interest in the link between child and parental well-being.

Denise Watson, Infant Physiotherapist
Denise Watson works in the infant physiotherapy unit at the Chelsea and Westminster Hospital, London.

Personal acknowledgements

Dr Rebecca Chicot
I would like to thank my parents, Katrina and Brian; my siblings, Daniel and Katie; and my own growing family: Rufus, Miranda, Benedict and Iris. Together you have confirmed my belief that the secret of happiness is family and you have supported me in my work at The Essential Parent Company that supports new parents and their families. Thanks also to Professor Winston for sharing his huge wealth of wisdom and experience in the fields of fertility, pregnancy and baby development.

Diana Hill
I would like to thank my son, Oscar, for inspiring the creation of The Essential Parent Company. I would also like to thank my husband, Shawn, for his ongoing patience and support and my wonderful parents, Elizabeth and Douglas. Thanks to the 'Bright Birds' for their ideas! Last and not least I would like to thank 'Prof' Robert Winston for being such an inspiring, generous and wonderful mentor and collaborator.

Together, we would like to thank our four extraordinary investors, Robert Clarke, Ralph Kanter, John Spearman and Hyman Bielsky, who have continued to believe in our work over the years. Without their financial, intellectual, creative and emotional support, this project would never have happened. Finally, thanks to Victoria Marshallsay for being such a patient and thoughtful editor.

Genesis Research Trust

www.genesisresearchtrust.com

Despite countless breakthroughs in medical science, we still do not understand why some pregnancies will end in tragedy. For most of us, having a child of our own is the most fulfilling experience of our lives. All of us can imagine the desperation and sadness of parents who lose a baby, and the life-shattering impact that a disabled or seriously ill child has on a family.

Led by Professor Robert Winston, the Genesis Research Trust raises money for the largest UK-based collection of scientists and clinicians who are researching the causes and cures for conditions that affect the health of women and babies. This trust is uniquely based in the building where the scientists carry out their research at the Wolfson and Weston Research Institute for Family Health, on the Hammersmith Campus of Imperial College London.

The objectives of the trust are to provide financial assistance for medical research and teaching in the field of gynaecology, obstetrics and related fields in paediatrics. The trust is organised in order to promote, by all available means, the study of healthy childbearing and diseases of women. Our teaching programme is internationally recognised and the work produced has the highest reputation among academics and researchers. Our courses and symposia are attended by approximately 3,000 full- and part-time students per year.

Advances in the well-being of women and babies can only be achieved by research into the disorders that can affect anyone. Our primary aim is to improve the health of the unborn child and its mother.

The Essential Parent Company

www.essentialparent.com

If you would like more information about our company and the fertility, pregnancy, birth and baby-care online courses we create, please visit our website.